THE REMNANT

Living in Triumph

THE
REMNANT

Living in Triumph

Priscilla Degnan Fritz

Whitaker House

Unless otherwise indicated, all Scripture quotations are from the *New International Version of the Bible*, © 1973, 1978, 1984 by the International Bible Society. Used by permission.

Scripture quotations marked (KJV) are from the King James Version of the Bible.

Scripture quotations marked (NAS) are from the *New American Standard Bible*, © 1960, 1962, 1968, 1971, 1973, 1975, 1977 by The Lockman Foundation. Used by permission.

Scripture quotations marked (RSV) are from the *Revised Standard Version Common Bible* © 1973, by the Division of Christian Education of the National Council of Churches of Christ in the U.S.A. Used by permission.

Scripture quotations marked (TLB) are from *The Living Bible*, © 1971 by Tyndale House Publishers, Wheaton, Illinois. Used by permission.

Excerpt from *The Body,* by Chuck Colson, 1992, Word Publishers, Nashville, Tennessee, used by permission. All rights reserved.

THE REMNANT: LIVING IN TRIUMPH

For speaking engagements:
Priscilla Fritz
Discipleship and Evangelism WorldWide
P.O. Box 18370
Reno, Nevada 89511
1-800-313-3399
www.dewwministry.com

ISBN: 0-88368-546-9
Printed in the United States of America
Copyright © 1998 by Whitaker House

Whitaker House
30 Hunt Valley Circle
New Kensington, PA 15068

1 2 3 4 5 6 7 8 9 10 11 12 / 08 07 06 05 04 03 02 01 00 99 98

Contents

Dedication...7

Preface 9

1. Seeking and Searching.................................11

2. Since the Garden 27

3. The Gatherings..53

4. Designer God 85

5. I Promise to Gather You.............................109

6. God Is Faithful 125

7. Who Will Be Counted His?.........................149

8. The Church..183

9. Living in Triumph......................................201

10. Triumph and Action..................................225

11. Search No More 233

For the faithful Remnant hearts,
who are the beloved of God

also

For those who are seeking
truth and peace,

May He carry you on
His wings.

(Exodus 19:4)

Preface

"'And what is [God]?' I asked the earth, and it answered me, 'I am not He.' Everything that is in it confessed the same. I asked the sea and the deeps and the living creeping things, and they answered, 'We are not your God; seek above us.' I asked the wind, and the whole atmosphere with his inhabitants answered, 'Anaximenes was deceived, I am not God.' I asked the heavens, sun, moon, and stars. They answered, 'Nor are we the God whom you seek.' And I replied to all my bodily senses, 'You have told me of my God, that you are not He; tell me something of Him.' And they cried out with a loud voice, 'He made us.' I questioned them in my thinking about them, and their form of beauty gave the answer. And I turned to myself and said to myself, 'Who are you?' I answered, 'A man.' And behold I perceived that I am made up of both soul and body, one outside, the other within. By which of these should I seek my God? I had sought Him in the body from earth to heaven, as far as I could send messengers—the beams of my eyes. But the inner is the better of the two. For to it, as if it were presiding and judging, all the bodily messengers reported the answers of heaven and earth and all things in them, who said, 'We are not God, but He made us.' My inner man perceived these things by the ministry of the outer. I, the inner man, knew them; I, the mind, knew them through the senses of my body. I asked the whole frame of the world about my God, and it answered me,

'I am not He, but He made me.'"

—Saint Augustine[1]

---

[1] *The Confessions of Saint Augustine* (New Kensington, PA: Whitaker House, 1996), pp. 251–252.

Chapter 1

Seeking and Searching

H e never knew who he was." Biff, Willie Loman's son, stood at his father's grave summing up Willie's life.[1] In his play, *Death of a Salesman*, Arthur Miller wrote about all those who seek peace, success, and purpose from this world. The gods of money, social significance, and personal recognition will not answer their prayers. Like Willie Loman, many of us have perhaps missed the real reason for life. Many of us have asked ourselves throughout our earthly journey, "Who am I, and why am I here?"

No one needs to be tossed around in confusion, grasping at man's attempts to satisfy these questions. Your earthly life is meant to be lived in peace, security, and inner power. You are a unique treasure, filled with special gifts. Life can have order and purpose and be lived in triumph. The goal is to discover how you can live in peace, security, and power.

I believe women and men are seeking and longing for a reason for their existence. I believe many have faulty pictures of

God in their minds. I believe many are living in bondage to their past.

This book was written to encourage these men and women to become a people of God, "The Remnant." It provides an overall look at God and our relationship with Him. It was also written to emphasize the importance of applying the Word and His moral laws to our daily lives.

Change is an exciting opportunity for the human race, yet many of us want to cling to whatever we find comfortable. As surely as the sun rises on a new day and the tides of the sea change continually, God has designed you to change.

Being too comfortable can stunt us emotionally and spiritually. A personal change for our good can seem uncomfortable, a struggle. We can defeat ourselves before we start, forgetting that He knows we will triumph. Struggles are learning grounds.

A parent shared this story with me, and I was immediately reminded of how our loving God leads His beloved child:

> "Why do we have to do this? It's too hard! Can't we just turn back? My legs hurt; I can't go another step!" All this was pleaded by our 9-year-old Sami on our way to our local mountain, Mount Rose, in September. But once she got to the top, she proudly beamed, "That wasn't so bad; now I feel like I could do anything!" Yeah Sami! She got it. As parents, it's a wonderful thing to watch your children "get it." And we adults are no different. The journey of life is a series of mountaintops and valleys and lots of flatland. And each time we face another challenge, we have options—complain and quit, grumble and inch slowly, or move forward anticipating growth.[2]

God wants you to know who you are. He never meant for you and me to wander in uncertainty. He has given you a plan of life. Living His way is living in peace, strength, and power. You can know who you are.

The Remnant

A remnant, according to *Webster*, is defined as "a small remaining part or number of persons. A last remaining indication of what has been."[3] God has promised to preserve a Remnant for Himself. The Word of God shows He is steadfast in His promise. For example:

> *But God sent me ahead of you to preserve for you a Remnant on earth.* (Genesis 45:7)

Preserving acts of God have continuously kept the Remnant. The Greek word *hupoleimma* (Isaiah 10:22–23, Romans 9:27) refers to a Remnant, where the contrast is drawn between the number of Israel as a whole and the number of those who are saved through the Gospel.[4] God the Father saved us through the sacrifice of His Son, God Jesus (John 3:16).

> *Though the number of the Israelites be like the sand by the sea, only the Remnant will be saved.* (Romans 9:27)

The term "people of Israel" refers to God's chosen people both then and now. He, through Christ, made it possible for all of us to become a people of Israel. He calls personally to you to be gathered to Him.

Throughout the Bible, God speaks of a Remnant people, His Israel. This Remnant can be described as a small remaining number of people throughout the centuries who have their hearts fully committed to Him. These are the children of His promise—the man, woman, or child who receives showers of His blessing (Psalm 68:9); protection under His mighty wing (Psalm 36:7); security, peace, and life forever (John 3:16).

Does God call to the Remnant today? Has there been a continuous link throughout the history of mankind, a link called the Remnant? Yes! The God of Abraham, Isaac, and Jacob made this promise:

> *For out of Jerusalem will come a Remnant, and out of Mount Zion a band of survivors. The zeal of the Lord Almighty will accomplish this.*   (2 Kings 19:31)

Who is God, the Lord Almighty? He is the Triune God, called the Holy Trinity, and consists of the Father, Son, and Holy Spirit. The Trinity is a three-in-one God with unique attributes. For those who struggle in their understanding of the Trinity, these analogies may help clarify this truth:

God the *Father* as a Root.
God the *Son* as a Branch.
God the *Holy Spirit* as the Fruit.

or this concept:

God the *Father* being the Sun.
God the *Son* being the Rays.
God the *Holy Spirit* being the Heat.

We live as His people in our world, our Jerusalem. Will you be gathered to Him as a Remnant? This is the plan for you, beloved reader. There is an offer made by the Triune God, the Father, Son, and Holy Spirit. It is His covenant offer.

Taken in covenant relationship, the extended hand of God offers you a life of confident excitement and power-filled purpose. Your life, when fully given to God, is a yielded life. When you live in obedient agreement with His moral laws, you live in covenant relationship.

A covenant is a binding or solemn agreement made between two individuals or parties.[5] A covenant relationship, offered to you by God, means that both enter into the agreement. His promises are for the person who agrees to live in heart obedience to God.

The Covenant

God has made great covenant agreements with us as His people. These covenants are found throughout His Word. The Remnant can stand on these promises and believe that God has not made them lightly or only for the ancient times. He does not and will not fail us. The history of mankind is one long lifeline of covenant relationships.

The covenant promises God made to Abraham (Genesis 12, 15, 17) and David (2 Samuel 7) were made to them as future promises. As God has kept these promises, we see the generations of the line of Abraham continuing on through the Remnant today. He kept His covenant with David by sending the King of Kings, Jesus Christ, from the line of David, as our eternal King.

Consider that God said He made you in His image (Genesis 1:26). It follows, then, that He created you to share in His holiness. Your response to God determines the empowering of your life. Your life, day by day, will be full, enriched, blessed and joy-filled when lived according to God's purpose. Choices apart from God lead to a self-willed life.

What meaning does this have to your next 24 hours or to the remaining number of days you will be given on this earth? That question is answered by realizing that when God, through Moses, made a covenant with the people of Moses after they were delivered from Egyptian slavery, it was a two-way agreement. God has said to you, "I will..." He will bring blessings to your life, but your response must be to make and uphold the covenant with Him. God has promised, *"...if you obey Me"* (Exodus 19:5).

How can this be possible? Jeremiah 31:33 affirms just how wonderful, how intimate your God is. *"I will put My law in their minds and write it on their hearts. I will be their God, and they will be My people."*

God has also initiated this New Covenant with you through Jesus Christ, who has made it possible for the moral laws of God to be written on your heart. A heart cry to Him allows the Holy Spirit to change your heart and to open your eyes. Opened hearts and eyes understand God and thirst to know Him. They trust God and want to become covenant keepers. A life process begins as a Remnant relationship is built through the power of the Holy Spirit.

God has made a covenant (Remnant) relationship possible. You can relate to God because His grace and His mercy have been poured out by Jesus Christ (John 3:16). God's love is received, and your heart obedience is now through the death of Jesus. You can now be made righteous through an inner transformation. Obedience is a love response to God's love for you.

Biblical covenants are understood through the knowledge of the types of royal covenants or treaties executed in the ancient Near East. Following are descriptions of the major covenants found in the Bible:

1. **Royal Grant**: Examples: God's commitments made to Noah (Genesis 9:8–17), Abraham (Genesis 15:9–21), Phinehas (Numbers 25:10–13), David (2 Samuel 7:5–16), Israel (New Covenant, Jeremiah 31:31–34).

This is an unconditional covenant given by the King (such as a land grant) for faithfulness, loyalty, and service. Heirs of the recipient benefited as long as they continued in faithfulness, loyalty and service.

2. **Suzerain-vassal**: Examples: Abraham (Genesis 17), Sinaitic (Exodus 19–24). This defines the relationship between a

great king and one of his subject kings. The great king is sovereign. Total loyalty and service (love) is demanded of the vassal. If the vassal is absolutely faithful and loyal, the great king gives him and his realm protection. The relationship is known as lord and servant or father and son. *"You yourselves have seen what I did to Egypt, and how I carried you on eagles' wings and brought you to Myself. Now if you obey Me fully and keep My covenant, then out of all nations you will be My treasured possession"* (Exodus 19:4–5).

3. **Parity**: This is a solemn agreement between equals. *"So Abraham brought sheep and cattle and gave them to Abimelech, and the two men made a treaty"* (Genesis 21:27). An oath was usually verbal and was officially given with gods called upon to witness the agreement. If the covenant was violated, curses would follow.

Living in covenant relationship with God is made possible for you through the power of the Holy Spirit. God's ways become written on your heart. Zechariah 7:9–10 points out the four tests of a believer's covenant relationship:

1. Administer true justice.
2. Show mercy and compassion to one another.
3. Do not oppress the widow, the fatherless, the alien or the poor.
4. Do not think evil of each other.

The Remnant believer seeks God to empower his or her heart and actions in order to live in covenant relationship.

Why live as a faithful Remnant woman or man? You can rest in His promises to be believed, His promises kept and His promises lived during a life designed for you by the great God

Almighty. Promises to a Remnant are given because of God's integrity. *"Now you, brothers, like Isaac, are children of promise"* (Galatians 4:28).

In order to believe this, you have to become familiar with the character of God. Otherwise, God is interpreted according to your guesswork or opinion.

I have searched to, first, discover who God has said He is. Secondly, I wanted to discover why God has, for thousands of years, remained in relationship with a world that has rebelled and worshipped other gods. Why would a holy God remain in faithful relationship with man after the first rebellion in the Garden of Eden? History, both secular and biblical, depicts man as self-willed and sin-filled. Is God going to be faithful in His love today? Will He endure us much longer? Why?

From childhood, I have sought the truth through reliable sources, experts, experiences, and facts. My question persisted, "Why would God put up with the hatred and violence and destruction acted out by mankind?" I began to search both in churches and books for an answer.

Biblical records reveal many lives in rebellion against God and a failure to love Him. God, after all, being God, could have easily turned away in anger or disgust and destroyed the earth.

I found that man could not answer my questions, except to offer possible explanations of God as each saw Him. Where could I discover His truth? The answer was, and is, to seek God Himself through prayer and revelation in His Word.

Racing to the Return

Why is it important today for you to understand your relationship with God? I believe we are racing toward the day of the return of Jesus Christ. The Bible has told us, for thousands of years, that this day is coming. The Messiah, Jesus Christ, will return and reign.

The Remnant will not be stopped by the coming battle of Armageddon; they will live with Him. The day of the Lord is the time when Christ will be seen and known to you as the victorious Lord of this world:

> *"Shout and be glad....For I am coming, and I will live among you," declares the Lord. "Many nations will be joined with the Lord in that day and will become My people. I will live among you."*   (Zechariah 2:10–11)

History continues to prove that biblical prophecy is accurate and true. The biblical prophets and apostles spoke to their contemporaries. They speak to you and me today with both warnings and strengthening promises.

Jesus Christ's return will permanently change mankind and all life—an exciting, revealing, and powerful event. The Remnant, God's faithful, should be eagerly anticipating this glorious day. God warns, however, that for the unfaithful it will be a day of darkness (Amos 5:18).

Millions of people on this earth today are seeking answers to the future in cults, mysticism and psychics. The future has been written, dear reader, by the One who is Truth—God the Father, Son, and Holy Spirit. Time is not measured by a world clock. God's time line and plan for the earth and for you and me has not changed since the Garden or since creation.

Throughout the centuries, people have heard that God loves His people and has called them to His kingdom. The Remnant has heard and believed. This kingdom news has been passed down generation after generation, first by accurate oral tradition, then by writings on stone and finally by the holy, revealed, written Word.

First-century Remnant believers, those who believed in the life, death, and resurrection of God Jesus Christ, were linked to the early prophets by faith. Believers knew the prophecy was fulfilled, and they spread the truth. *"The kingdom of heaven has been forcefully advancing, and forceful men lay hold of it"* (Matthew 11:12).

Others heard and scoffed at God, and this is still so today. Bowing down to man-made gods of convenience or power is not new. Others heard and worshipped at the altars of darkness. Others simply ignored God, not bothering to take the time to go to His revealed Word, the place to discover Him for themselves.

A gathering of these "others" at the throne of God will be a gathering of those *"weeping and gnashing [their] teeth"* (Matthew 8:12). Tears will surely stream down the face of the Savior Jesus. He will have to address the multitudes who worshipped themselves. Jesus wept over Jerusalem for the same reason. He knew what they had missed:

> *If you, even you, had only known on this day what would bring you peace—but now it is hidden from your eyes.*
> (Luke 19:42)

The price for refusing His offer of life is severe, and at the time of His return, there will be no moment left in which to choose Him. This gathering will be at God's last judgment. All will have been decided before that appearance. Jesus Christ made it clear. They will be *"thrown outside, into the darkness, where there will be weeping and gnashing of teeth"* (Matthew 8:12).

I am amazed that anyone would reject His offer of a secure and intimate relationship. The Creator of all things and the One whose name is Love and Mercy makes that offer. Why would a man or woman choose not to have Him on his or her side in this lifetime?

Could it be that those who reject God simply do not know Him? I have heard many different descriptions about who God is and what God should be. It is as though God is a coloring book picture in the hands of a toddler with a box of crayons, a different image depending on the maturity of the child. The younger the child, the wilder and more distorted the picture, just as those who have little knowledge of the biblical God have drawn a distorted image of Him.

It is each person's responsibility to personally know God. Paul's letter to the Philippians prayerfully encouraged them:

> *And this is my prayer: that your love may abound more and more in knowledge and depth of insight, so that you may be able to discern what is best and may be pure and blameless until the day of Christ, filled with the fruit of righteousness that comes through Jesus Christ—to the glory and praise of God.* (Philippians 1:9–11)

Finding Him

Looking out into the darkness of the night, I could not make out the road ahead. Driving on an unfamiliar road to get to a speaking commitment is never a comfortable experience for me. Wondering what lay ahead, I longed for a little light that would make me feel a bit more safe until a familiar landmark or sign appeared. This is probably a common experience for many others who travel on a desolate road with a dark sky above and no horizon ahead.

But then, a glow to the east and a soft light appeared, becoming stronger and more brilliant until at last the sun burst over the mountaintop. Now I could clearly see the desert ahead for forty miles. My surroundings seemed safe now that nothing would suddenly leap out of the darkness. I felt peaceful because

I could see the roadway ahead. Dark shadows had become a friendly landscape.

This experience is similar to much of life. I need to see where I am going, and I need to have the light to do so. I walked through years of darkness, not knowing I was living a desolate life. Yet, I was longing for the true light.

I worked hard to succeed and achieve while gaining an education and became schooled in philosophy, history, and religion. Searching and seeking, my heart was like stone toward any talk of Jesus Christ. A God of love, in a world filled with hatred, war, abuse, and confusion, seemed illogical.

One day I finally realized I had been walking in the darkness of a thousand false suns. That day my heart was opened to the true Light of the World, God the Son Jesus Christ. I had been fiercely refusing His light for years. The light did not belong to a religion, a group, or even to the godly pastor speaking that day. I looked into the face of the Greatest Love, beyond human description. At last I could see God.

The Word of God I heard in a church became clear that day. The Father's love seemed to fill me beyond description. My heart accepted as fact that Jesus Christ had taken my sin upon Himself. I could be cleansed and could walk into the presence of a welcoming God. The Son Himself had risen, and I would forever be in the radiance of His glory. I was free of the darkness at last!

I didn't realize then that the Holy Spirit had been preparing my heart. God had chosen this moment to change my heart. He could hear my call to Him, even though I did not know to whom I was calling. I was found by Him, and I realized that my life apart from Him had been an empty dream. So I asked Jesus to forgive me, and I gave Him my life.

Until that time, I had, in my limited thinking, looked at life as a brief span to be lived well and enjoyed before it was over.

Was this the plight of man, who I thought was a product of some cosmic accident and evolutionary chance?

A poem by Henry Wadsworth Longfellow had been one of my favorites, but only the first stanza had ever captured my attention:

> Tell me not in mournful numbers
> Life is but an empty dream;
> For the soul is dead that slumbers
> And things are not what they seem.

However, *now* I saw the depth of what Longfellow wrote in the next stanza:

> Life is real! Life is earnest!
> And the grave is not its goal;
> Dust thou art, to dust returnest,
> Was not spoken of the soul.

Having chosen to surrender all to Jesus Christ, I experienced new life. However, I discovered that I had three unrealistic expectations. One, every person who claimed to believe in Jesus Christ would want to live fully for Him and find out as much about Him as they could. Two, I would find that churches that claimed to be Christ-centered would be filled with the radiance of God Himself. Three, the body, the people within a church, would be living in triumphant obedience.

The more I learned about the majesty, justice, faithfulness, and forgiveness of God, the more excited I became for everyone to find freedom and victory in Him. This was the answer for the confused and corrupt state of mankind, and it was all so simple.

The ancient Greek mathematician and inventor, Archimedes (c. 287–212 B.C.), was puzzled as he sought a solution to one particular problem. He was both wise and persevering. At last, the solution to the problem came to his mind. "Eureka!" he called out, which in English means, "I have found it!"

Eureka! This cry was also heard across our nation. Just west of the Sierra Nevada Mountains is a place called Sutter's Fort, California. In the 1840s a miner discovered gold in a creek owned by Sutter and cried, "Eureka!" This was a howl of delight for new riches found and now personally owned.

Eureka! When the American people heard that word, they began a race to the West, and the California Gold Rush was on. There was a promise of new life, with a fortune in gold just waiting to be found. That is how I felt and still feel today about the discovery that new life is available in Jesus Christ. Because God so loves you, He has left true gold in a stream of living water available to you.

Eureka! That is how I felt when, by the grace of God, faith was given to me and I believed. In one moment, my life changed completely. According to Ephesians 2:8–9, it was by God's favor toward me that He gave me the gift of knowing He is Truth.

Why would anyone choose not to leave everything behind and go for the gold? This golden offer to believe in His Son and to live in covenant relationship has been made by God. But the Living Water, Jesus, is often ignored and His gold remains in the water.

What is the present-day condition of man? I wondered if we as a world were simply becoming increasingly dependent upon technology and scientific answers. Have more options led to apathy and/or rejection of the Creator?

As a new believer and now as a believer of over twenty years, I agree with the simple fact that the Word of God is the most unchanged and historically true document since recorded history. The first time I heard this, I could not believe my ears. Surely, the high school and college history and science professors had not left out such an important fact. But yes, they had, and I had accepted for twenty-nine years that the Bible was simply an invention of a group of men with a cause. How many times I still encounter family and friends and strangers who believe the same thing. I know now this is a common tactic of Satan.

The counsel of God in Psalm 146:3–4 is wise. Do not put your life in the hands of false experts who know nothing of life, of salvation life. Mere humans don't have what it takes; when they die, their projects die with them. Instead, put your hope in God and know the real blessing.[6]

So much of my own searching for truth, sorting out relationships and striving for success during my years as an unbeliever had been in vain. How I had needed to listen to the tender voice of our mighty God speaking, "Priscilla, *'Be still, and know that I am God'* (Psalm 46:10)."

Beloved reader, have you been still? Have you listened with an open heart to the Holy Spirit? Do you know without reservation that HE IS GOD?

Notes

1. Arthur Miller, *Death of a Salesman* (New York: Penguin Books, 1976), p. 138.

2. K. Baldock, NV, 1996. Used with permission.

3. D. Guralink, ed., *Webster's New World Dictionary* (New York: Simon and Schuster, 1984), p. 1202.

4. W. E. Vine, *Vine's Expository Dictionary of Old and New Testament Words* (Grand Rapids: Revell, 1981), p. 276.

5. Guralink, *Webster's New World Dictionary,* p. 326.

6. Eugene Peterson, *The Message* (Colorado Springs: Navpress, 1995), p. 856.

Chapter 2

Since the Garden

Making Your Own Rules

Picture several family members sitting in church on a Sunday morning, each hoping to get a little of the "goodness of God" rubbed off on them. Then they rush out of their place of worship to spit out anger, selfishness, and greed, or maybe they just ignore God during the coming week.

Fathers ignore their wives and children while indulging themselves in careers, television sets, alcohol, drugs, and affairs. Mothers focus on meeting their own emotional needs by nagging, yelling, controlling, or ignoring. A father rules his family with killing words, demanding his own satisfactions be first. He is so weak that he rules by fear.

A woman engages in mental battles with a husband who has failed to lead the home as a man of God. She does not have to be loud and angry; she can express silent anger with equally disastrous results. Even as she serves in the ministry, on the church board, or as a volunteer in the schools and community, she uses her anger to control. Because she disobeys God, He becomes an abstract and distant part of her attempts to have her own needs met. Children, who never see a living example of the Lord in their young lives, seek approval and affirmation from the standards of darkness of the present age. Drugs, sexual activity, rebellion, and gangs are all sought out because of the emptiness that fills their home.

Going to church does not raise your family, nor does sending your children to Sunday school, expecting they will then understand how to live as a believer in a difficult world. Carrying the light of Christ involves knowing God and then igniting the hearts of those you love through example, prayer, and godly responsibility in relationships. You must yield your life for your partner and children, just as Christ did.

Imagine if today your husband or wife or children were asked to write down their knowledge of the Word. Was their knowledge learned by your life and sharing? If they were asked how they learned to stand on the promises of God for their lives, what would they answer? If they were asked how your life was evidence of God's character to them, how would they respond?

Perhaps they would say they had always thought the family had an "okay" relationship, because it was filled with many of the usual activities and family gatherings. Was it a family with involved parents who never brought God into their daily lives, perhaps?

Does your family trust the world as their source of power? Would they believe you worship at the altar of yourself? Have they been taught to worship at the frail altar of pleasure and success? A legacy of life, true life, should be the great witness of a parent's life.

What did the Lord God say about this?

He who trusts in the Lord will prosper. He who trusts in himself is a fool. (Proverbs 28:25–26)

Religion Called Self

Are you a dry tree that is not being watered by the Word and nourished by prayer and devotion? Are the branches of your life barren? Is this a season of restoring or refinement that you will not allow the Lord God to work out?

Worshipping the idol of personal success never results in the real success that is designed by God Almighty. That idol must be smashed in your spirit right now. If you are living in your own strength in any aspect of your life, you live in a dry season and on self-maintenance level.

Worshipping false idols is rather like standing at the top of a ski run, with skis in hand, waiting for a snowfall so you can fly down the mountainside. God has promised the storehouse of His bounty in season (Ezekiel 34:26). He knows when He will choose to fill the mountainside with snow so you can take action and have an excellent run.

Does God have to discipline areas of your life that might include your relationships with family, unforgiveness of others, or living for your own pleasure instead of service to God? Perhaps the Lord God is developing obedience and responsibility in this waiting season of your life.

You may feel you have all the right equipment to ski down the mountain, and sometimes you may have even taken advantage of artificial snow. However, only God can lower the temperature and send snow in season, so you can take a deep breath and enjoy every turn as you meet the challenge of skiing down a glorious, genuine, snow-packed mountainside.

Manipulative love relationships never last. They are weak humanly and spiritually. When one is threatened into a relationship, one defensively moves away from it. A relationship that is not built on one's own heart belief is built on air. Man cannot manipulate God. Worship of self is a religion without a relationship with God.

Lasting relationships are built day after day by spending intimate time together and experiencing promises kept. They are built on foundation stones of trust and truth. Intimate time shared daily with God results in a rock-solid relationship with Him. The only relationship with God that makes your life exhilarating is one where He is your only God.

Does absence make the heart grow fonder, as the old saying goes? Separation creates a deep longing. Separation from God weighs heavily on the heart of the Remnant believer. This is a yearning the Remnant believer experiences as a heart-hunger and thirst. It causes a person to want to draw closer to God, desiring intimacy with Him. Whoever is without God, I believe, is longing for Him.

Life built upon humans or deceptive feelings is shaky, an unstable house built on anxiety and self-dependence. Feeling more and more that you are separated from deep love, you long for more. This difficult and disturbing situation causes you heart pain. Self-dependence leads to disorder and a lack of unity in your relationship with God.

Feelings of alienation and loneliness and an inability to find an intimate relationship can cause much pain. Paul Meier, co-director of the outstanding Minirth-Meier Clinic, describes lack of intimacy as a problem resulting from "alienation from the love of God." He believes the answer to this problem is found in reconciliation with God and restoration through Him. "God loves people unconditionally, and through a relationship with God a person develops a sense of identity as God's somebody."[1]

Independent or Dependent

During the 1970s and 1980s, a "me" generation emerged in the United States. Interestingly enough, this emergence followed the fade-out generation of the 1960s, when moral codes and personal ethics eroded.

A high price was paid by many who faded away from productive lives and bought into a lie. Drugs became a common escape. A generation had moved from trusting God to trusting idols. An anonymous poem describes the results of a self-destruction that continues today. Tragically, the following is based on the great 23rd Psalm:

> King Heroin is my shepherd, I shall always want.
> He maketh me to lie down in the gutters,
> He leadeth me beside the troubled waters,
> He destroyeth my soul.[2]

King Heroin could be any idol that you are making king of your life.

In the 1970s, one issue of a reputable major magazine asked this bold question on its cover: *"Is God Dead?"* I thought He was at that time, but the question made me wonder about the condition of our society. People were alarmed.

A generation of young people began a major fade-out of social responsibility. Without the benefit of strong values and moral choices, they have raised new generations. A college professor at the time, I witnessed firsthand how drugs became the god of a generation. Many a fine young man or woman failed to learn how to resolve conflict and how to deal well with difficult times as well as good.

What was missing? Mostly, this generation was not being taught the moral and ethical codes of God. The role of the father as spiritual leader of the home was being abdicated. Slowly, slowly it progressed until an explosion of crime and chaos ruled. Frightening headlines seemed to become the norm in America. What used to be outrageous no longer seemed to cause any reaction. Murder, child rape and abuse, political corruption, drugs, and divorce were no longer the exception. We are living with the results of this today. We cease to be alarmed or surprised by rebellion against God's moral laws.

To be sure, those who continued to obey God's commands to train their young, uphold values and character, and model ethics in their lives still glued society together. Their battle was fierce and still is today.

The 1960s and 1970s may have left too many dropouts on the edge. In the 1980s education and success once again seemed to become important to the young, but drugs, divorce, and lack of moral codes still tore apart society. Now the young want success. New ethical codes have been put in place based on success, doing "one's own thing," and "whatever."

For the most part, God's spoken code of ethics was left in closed Bibles and ignored in spiritually dead churches. Important to note, however, was a new non-denominational revival in America that spoke to and saved thousands upon thousands for Christ. The Remnant survived; God was not dead. There is always a surviving Remnant of God during the darkest spiritual times.

Look into your heart. What do you value? The contrast is well defined by the following article:

> We value a man who is independent. God values a man dependent on Him. We value a man who marches to his own beat. God values a man who marches to His beat. We value a man who is his own authority, who makes up the rules as he goes along. God values a man who submits, who follows the ancient rules made by Another. We value a man who believes in himself, who makes himself great. God values a man who believes in Him, recognizing He alone is great.[3]

This writer makes it clear there is quite a difference between the lover of self and self-determination and the Remnant believer who loves God. Man bows down to the golden achievements of those who scoff at the Word and ethics of God, and he has determinedly shaped self as a golden idol over the past decades.

Man has propelled himself to seek the spiritism of what is now considered new age, the occult, and false religions. This idol has been a fashion in the recent history of the United States. Forming idols has opened the door to a blinded people, designing a god the way they have designed a home, a vacation, a family, and a religion.

One father, speaking to a friend, strongly declared that he does not believe he should attend church or take his family. Although he attentively takes them to many other activities, he makes his own rules about fellowship with God. This man has created a designer god no different than the ones the Israelites allowed to weaken their family lives thousands of years ago:

> *They did not destroy the peoples, as the Lord commanded them, but they mingled with the nations and learned to do as they did. They served their idols, which became a snare to them. They sacrificed their sons and their daughters to the demons.* (Psalm 106:34–37 RSV)

As recorded in the Old Testament, the most read book in the world, fathers who fail to live in covenant relationship with God have not blessed their families. God has given the father much responsibility in marriage and family. A father who does not have a relationship with God will find that the world system is waiting with gleeful arms to steal the morals and character of his wife and/or children.

The Old Testament books of Genesis, 1 and 2 Kings, and 1 and 2 Chronicles bear witness to the men who broke the covenant with God. These Bible books describe the effects on wives and children. Family pain, children in rebellion, destruction of nations, and God's anger upon the fathers are the results.

Just stories of ancient history? No. Look at the families today in which there is no God or where a designer god has been installed. What consequences are we able to see in these marriages and families? Divorce, conflict, addictions, and an inability to find purpose are just a few.

I asked this particular father about his refusal to honor God in a fellowship of believers and why he determined his own course. He made the excuse that the churches were full of people who didn't measure up.

No doubt our churches should be filled with Remnant people, but that is not a reason to forsake gathering to worship God. To be sure, the consequences of his disobedience will be felt in every one of his relationships. He has already left a trail of unhappiness.

God is God, and He doesn't make a special ruling for an arrogant heart. God is, however, always waiting to make Himself known. Ancient, powerful Babylon thought it was able to maintain its own throne after defeating the house of Jacob and Israel. Hear what God says to those who make their own rules about Him:

> *You have trusted in your wickedness and have said, "No one sees me." Your wisdom and knowledge mislead you when you say to yourself, "I am, and there is none besides me." Disaster will come upon you, and you will not know how to conjure it away.* (Isaiah 47:10–11)

Incomparable Power

The Remnant, however, trusts the true God and holds up His standard as the guideline for family and personal life. For several years I have had a very close relationship with a dear friend. As she has raised a family, I have been part of that family as well.

She and her husband live out their belief in His faithfulness day in and day out. I am always encouraged to witness their trust in God. Decisions for themselves and their children are made in the presence of God. All the normal confrontations and joys of marriage, children, and personal growth take place in their home. The Lord is the center of their lives.

My friend, actually my sister in Christ, has always held me accountable to God as well. In faithful prayer times, we both have experienced God's protective guidance and love over the past several years. Both of us can trust each other with our deepest struggles, because we know the other can be trusted. Just as we have learned we can absolutely trust God, He joins our hearts together as well. This relationship is a precious gift, one in which we find Jesus is the center. We know that God has given us the one heart of John 17:21.

> *For this reason, ever since I heard about your faith in the Lord Jesus and your love for all the saints, I have not stopped giving thanks for you, remembering you in my prayers. I pray...that you may know...His incomparably great power for us who believe.*
>
> (Ephesians 1:15–16, 18–19)

This precious woman agreed to share this story about herself in the hope that other lives would be encouraged in the Lord.

How had this Remnant woman decided to live for God? "I had just recovered from an abortion and was in despair of the sin. My mother came to me with a book about prayer, and she prayed with me. From that point, I began to seek the Lord like never before. It seemed like a slow process, but healing was taking place. I had at last recognized that choosing my own way continually resulted in personal disaster."

When she and I met at a wonderful Christian teaching retreat in North Carolina, she was certainly walking in her new commitment to Jesus Christ and was a beautiful, radiant woman. Since that time she has married a godly man, and they are raising their family according to God the Father, Son, and Holy Spirit. I pray that those who ignore God and His morality will be blessed by knowing such a family.

In response to my questions for this book, she said that indeed she prayed daily and wanted to continue to grow in the way she submits to God. She longs to see others around her saved and secure through Jesus Christ, "because I love them and want them to know the peace and happiness that I enjoy."

The Word of God very much influences her relationships with her husband and children. About her marriage, she said, "We both know the Lord brought us together. When troublesome situations arise, we turn to God for direction." This is a woman who recognizes that her children belong to God, and she is responsible to Him for her parenting choices. Both she and her husband share the Word and pray with the children daily. "I am convicted by the Holy Spirit if I am choosing my own ways in discipline or other situations. I then allow the Lord to teach me the best choices."

As a woman of God, she witnesses to many in the workplace who are unaware of God. She is a light and a witness to her female friends, as God is a priority in her relationships. "I witness and pray for my friends. I share the Bible's perspective as gently as I can. I am saddened by how many I have known who have been taken in by the world."[4]

This woman has many interests and a delightful personality. She is a mother, a successful career woman, and a servant of the Lord. Those who love God always touch other people's lives.

Those who love God serve Him by serving others. She has been called to serve God through discipleship. Many lives have been changed by witnessing her faithfulness to God's command to disciple (Matthew 28:19).

Women and men who live to return God's love and walk according to His moral laws are the Remnant who testify to the Word of God's truth today.

False Gods

Rebellion has been in our nature since the Garden of Eden. From the beginning, men and women have turned their hearts from God to themselves, even though His perfect provision was made for them. Making one's own god has been a stumbling block to both men and women ever since.

"Oh, astrology is all right. After all, God made the stars," said one serious young man who considered himself to be quite mature in the Word. He claimed it was quite harmless to accept that a star sign influences your personality and your destiny. It is not harmless to suggest that a believer's life could be influenced by the charting of the stars and moon and sun.

God poured out His wrath on the Israelites in Canaan because they worshipped heavenly bodies and made shrines to the star of the god Rephan (Acts 7:43). They listened to the twisted words of the deceiver. It is evident that the same ears that listened to Satan in the Garden have kept on listening to deception. Today man is worshipped; churches are worshipped; the stars, psychics, and relationships are worshipped. All are idols.

An idol is spoken of in the Scriptures, using a number of Hebrew and Greek words. The Old Testament Hebrew and Greek meanings of the word *idol* include:

1. An abstract expression, in deep moral terms, of the degradation associated with idols. Some of the Hebrew and Greek words protest the enormity of idols of the people.
2. Words which apply to the images as outward symbols of a designed deity.[5]

In abstract terms an idol is called an "empty thing" *(Heb. awen)*, such as vanity and wickedness. It also connotes wickedness in a moral sense—a vain, false, or wicked thing. The word aptly expresses the natural consequences of idol worship.[6]

Idolatry is classified as the paying of divine honors to any created thing. An example is how Israel, in the course of her history, adopted the idolatrous practice from her heathen neighbors. These included the gods of Egypt, Canaan, Babylonia, and Assyria.[7]

If we look deep within ourselves, we will find that in the past, or to this day, created things have held a place of worship in our lives. It is critical that we remove them from our personal altars now. Have you placed a new home, car, clothes, or travel as gods in your life? Do you sacrifice your children at the altar of wants? Worry and anxiety can be your idol if your trust is not in God alone, but in self to solve a problem.[8]

The Remnant worships only at the throne of the Creator, the God of Abraham, Isaac, and Jacob. Only Jesus Christ is to be served as the Savior God:

I am the Lord your God, who brought you out of Egypt, out of the land of slavery. You shall have no other gods before Me. (Exodus 20:2–3)

You shall not make for yourself an idol in the form of anything in heaven above or on the earth beneath or in the waters below. You shall not bow down to them or worship them; for I, the Lord your God, am a jealous God. (Exodus 20:4–5)

These are the first two commandments of the ten given to Moses for you and me on Mount Sinai. God has not changed. The consequences of ignoring His commands will still take place. Consequences in our own lives and in our family's lives will result. God will not tolerate wickedness.

Are you experiencing failure, frustrations, stress, and confusion? Go to a quiet place and ask the Holy Spirit to reveal the gods you have installed in your mind and heart. Ask Jesus to change your heart and mind about them. Trust Him to be faithful, forgiving, and empowering.

Loving us with patience beyond human capability, God is both for us and with us. He will make both Himself and His directions known to us when we ask Him. However, too frequently, those who are seeking God hope to avoid His directions by turning their hearts back to their Egypt. They seek man-made idols carved of stone, wood, or glass, or they seek the stars that were created by God for His particular purpose. They're really choosing to loose the darkness of Lucifer himself in their lives:

> *How you have fallen from heaven, O morning star, son of the dawn! You have been cast down to the earth.*
> (Isaiah 14:12)

Gaining a Foothold

Looking to live a Remnant life? Beware of opening doors to emotional pitfalls. The forces of darkness are empowered by actions and reactions outside of God's laws. A spirit of evil begins to gain a foothold within. For example, Paul, speaking of anger, emphatically warns us not to give the Devil a foothold (Ephesians 4:27). Danger signals shriek out warnings, but darkness covers your ears and your heart. God expresses His righteous anger at sin by dealing with us when we design our own gods, compromise His moral law, or worship at our own altars.

Paul, in his letter to the Ephesians, warns of the dangers of lying, getting angry, stealing, and tearing down through speech (Ephesians 4:25–29). These actions are an opportunity for Satan to separate a believer's heart and mind from God.

An angry person usually sees life only as it applies to himself or herself. Needing to make a point with loud, out-of-control retorts are common if one feels infringed upon. The angry person feels criticized, isolated and out of control. The problem is that relationships are broken by anger. Will Rogers once made this wise statement: "People who fly into a rage always make a bad landing."[9]

Why does explosive anger seem to have a particular hold on a person under any stress or pressure? Our hearts are exposed under stress. God often allows these tests so the false heart is revealed. Jesus did not pull defensive verbal power plays when He was being brutalized and was suffering on the cross. He could endure with a heart of peace, because He knew who He was.

The Christian who is a Remnant believer bears up well under pressure, because the Holy Spirit is within. The spirit of God is a spirit of peace. Who wants to be around an angry, explosive person? No one. Anger is not respected and a temper tantrum is seen as childish. Violence is actually weakness—a method of expressing hurt inappropriately. Godly fellowship is delightful, strong, comforting, encouraging, and serving.

On occasion there could be a situation that certainly does call for righteous anger, because God has been insulted. However, an explosive, uncontrolled temper usually erupts due to a lack of self-esteem. Explosive behavior is sinful because it selects a target for one's lack of self-control. This results from a need for self to be exalted because of a sense of being powerless. What is the reason for this? This person is not in a heart, covenant relationship with God the Father, Son, and Holy Spirit.

The angry person does not believe in or does not receive personal security in the arms of God. An unchanged heart exists within that person. Many people make an idol of anger deep inside themselves. We have all probably known a person with a seemingly calm exterior, whose anger is expressed subtly by retaliating against a husband, wife, or child. It may be in rage or in soft-spoken daggers, but the fact is that: *"Out of the abundance of the heart the mouth speaketh"* (Matthew 12:34 KJV).

Walking in the presence of God, as a Remnant, does not mean that you are always living on happy street. We are all tested daily by stress and pressure. How we handle it reflects our relationship with God. At no time does God give us permission to vent with angry, hurtful words. This is sin.

Often an angry person becomes more angry because he or she loses control over situations. Robbing the peace of others is outside of God's will. Confrontation, of course, in an appropriate manner, is what Jesus Christ modeled. Sometimes He confronted others firmly. Jesus was angry at sin, but His responses were appropriate. Learning to deal with anger by not letting it harbor or letting *"the sun go down"* on it (Ephesians 4:26) frees the Remnant believer from actual bondage. Another person or situation must never disturb the peace of Christ that lives in the heart of the Remnant. Aristotle made this observation:

> Anybody can become angry—that is easy; but to be angry with the right person and to the right degree, and at the right time, and for the right purpose, and in the right way—that is not within everybody's power and it is not easy.[10]

Aristotle, you certainly got that right! However, remember that Aristotle did not have the righteousness of Jesus Christ within him. You and I have the option to choose Christ, and He changes us. It is within our power today to break the chains of anger. Remnant believers grow to understand this, and they call on the Holy Spirit and Jesus to lift their hearts to Him and to turn anger to peace.

Beloved reader, I have seen anger hold onto a person with fiery clamps, which allows Satan to step right up to claim a mind. He twists and turns until the mind burns with imaginings. The mind develops a whole scenario as to the thoughts and feelings of the object of its anger. It consumes time and energy, and the angry person indeed makes a bad landing, as Will Rogers said.

Not long ago a young man came to my office. He was very upset about his lack of power in his leadership role. He felt he should be making decisions that truly were the responsibility of the ministry leader. His anger at his leader spilled out with criticism and manipulation. He sought out others who were associated with the leader to complain, condemn, and harass.

During this time, his anger and vengefulness were enveloping him, causing illness. The problem was other ears were listening to his sinful anger, infecting God's work with inaccurate judgments. The young man will perhaps grow to maturity one day under the discipline of God.

Ministries, churches, workplaces, and families have experienced the same frustrating attacks. The Devil delights in man's lust of the flesh and eyes. However, God's purposes are never thwarted by angry or jealous men or women. God did not allow this young man to prosper in that particular ministry. He was asked to leave the group, to take time to reflect on God's will for him.

Prayer, the Word, and the Holy Spirit began to open this young man's heart. After many months he began to realize that when God has called a godly pastor or godly leader, the enemy will scheme to destroy him or her. Satan is the enemy who gains a foothold through anger in anyone's life. The enemy looks for an opening to harass the work of the Lord. The young man began to understand this as he allowed himself to feel more and more thwarted, which resulted in envy. That sin led to his believing his own lies. Much prayer and guidance in the truth was needed. By allowing Jesus to rework his heart, he began to be restored. Satan lost the foothold of jealousy and anger.

Sometimes a person is not willing to repent for being self-willed. God, I believe, allows a person to stew until he or she accepts His way. Fortunately, this young man recognized the personal danger he was in and began to repent. Separation from God gave him no peace. He found peace only in his restored intimacy with God.

This present life is being lived in the midst of bewildering amounts of information and influences. New generations have not even heard about Jesus Christ or the Bible. Moral laws and ethical choices never even surface in their hearts. Many are raised in families with the ethics of parents who serve themselves, while others are brought up with no concept of the rewards of moral character.

Often, I am on planes racing across the polar route to Europe to speak or teach for Discipleship and Evangelism WorldWide. On these eleven-hour flights, two feature movies are shown. Almost always I try to sleep or finish work. However, the scenes shown on the screens are unavoidable unless I put on an eye mask and sleep. Now and again I will catch glimpses of a current top adventure film, usually with one actor who has gained popularity through violent and destructive plots.

The passengers are what draw my attention. Many are paying rapt attention to the movie-made strength of a heroic figure blasting away lives and buildings. The lead actor seems to be unstoppable and fearless in impossible circumstances. Those whose eyes are completely focused on the screen are having the strength of man imprinted into their thought processes.

Could a man be dreaming that he, too, could be as strong and fearless? Could he be thinking that his own life is rather drab? Is it possible that a woman is dreaming that her ideal would be to have this seemingly strong male in her life? Is she thinking that she would be fulfilled and happy if she looked like or became one of the female characters?

On one particular trip I was disturbed by the total concentration of a young boy. He was caught up in a movie world of violence and sexual immorality. Could that child be setting his heart on becoming a "terminator" or whomever? I silently prayed for this child and his parents sitting beside him. They obviously saw no problem with the teaching their child was absorbing.

Throughout the country, our teens and even six-year-old children are killing and beating each other. At first, it's a horrifying fact, but then men, women, and families who have killer heroes begin to assimilate it into an everyday occurrence.

The front page headlines in bold large print announced: 1996 AMA Report: TV MAYHEM STIRS KIDS' VIOLENCE. This press report stated that doctors of the American Medical Association in the *Physicians' Guide to Media Violence* stated, "Media violence is partly responsible for a rise in teenage crime."[11]

Children in gangs throughout many nations are taking drugs and raping and beating each other in record numbers. Why should the American Medical Association have to counsel us about entertaining our children with violence? My concern is that parents are neglecting or rejecting their children because they themselves have a crumbling, unworkable code of ethics.

The Washington Post reported the results of a 1997 survey. Nearly three-fourths of the murders of children in the industrialized world occur in the United States. Out of 2,872 estimated homicides and suicides of children in the world's richest nations, the following was found:

- 73 percent of homicides: U.S. children
- 54 percent of suicides: U.S. children
- 86 percent of deaths caused by guns: U.S. children[12]

As a nation we seem to have lost the ability or desire to live with a code of ethics that will prosper the child, individual, family, or community.

The AMA report continued to note that among 13- to 17-year-olds, violent crime has climbed 126 percent from 1976 to 1992, and TV and movie violence are partly responsible.[13]

Violent movies, books about the occult, witchcraft, and drugs are all holding more and more allure for the vacant lives of today. What has happened? In the past decades, as social and political revolutions have taken place, the standards of God have been lost. Parents' and children's heroes have become the violent, sexually impure, and morally dead figures of the media—all seeking life at the altars of evil. When we soak our minds with what we see and hear, the Lord's ethics become a distant memory.

Yet, I have heard some of the same people say that the crucifixion of Jesus Christ is too bloody of an event to personally accept. These are the same men and women who accept the violent and immoral on-screen behavior of their fictional heroic saviors. The idea that our own sin cost Jesus Christ His life painfully convicts us. However, His payment for sin (His spilled blood) was out of love.

On screen, the media's and society's heroes are weak heroes. No strength can compare to the strength of the Hero of 2,000 years ago, the Silent Sufferer, the Burden Bearer, whose compassion opened the gates of heaven.

Becoming familiar with the biblical model of life teaches us that anything and everything in life is possible only through Almighty God. We are becoming accustomed to believing that strength is in human power. That danger looms in the mind-set of a society that looks to man.

This Present Life: Struggles of the Stranger

A Remnant believer recognizes that his or her life belongs to God:

> *You have made my days a mere handbreadth; the span of my years is as nothing before you. Each man's life is but a breath....For I dwell with you as an alien, a stranger, as all my fathers were.* (Psalm 39:5, 12)

The Psalmist realized life on this earth is but a pilgrimage, that of a stranger passing through on a journey (Psalm 84:5). In the days of one's youth, this could be a difficult concept. The very young often believe themselves to be invincible. The very young rarely think about the end of life.

The Remnant believer, however, knows from the moment of his or her faith in Jesus Christ that there will be no end of life. No one but God knows the length of our earthly journey. We can look through the Scriptures and find that thousands of lives briefly journeyed through their natural years. The life spans of Sarah (127 years), Abraham (175 years) and Moses (120 years) may seem long, relative to the thousands of years recorded in biblical history, but they are merely a heartbeat in time. Jesus Christ, who saved man from himself, lived only 33 years. If others were to look at a quick video playback of only the last year of our lives, what would they see?

The Bible reveals the lives of many diverse people. They did not have telephones, cars, or computers, but the Bible relates stories of their lives through the centuries. Do not dismiss them simply because they are ancient. They did not have a VCR or a camera to record history for us, so it was written in the Word. Today, it would be possible to videotape you twenty-four hours a day for the future generations. Would the book of your life record a Remnant testimony or something quite different?

Every day upon waking, you can rejoice that the Lord has made this day for you. *"Rejoice in the Lord always....Rejoice!"* (Philippians 4:4). Your day may include a difficult struggle. Today, for example, you may be struggling with the consequences of yesterday's choices. Are you willing to allow God to direct your path? Through that trial, the Lord God is making Himself known to you, drawing you closer to Him. Does your mind translate to your heart that *"this is the day the Lord has made; let us rejoice and be glad in it"* (Psalm 118:24)?

Ask God to put His shield around you. No enemy can get through God's protection. I assure you, you will be filled with wonder as you feel God's presence. You will be filled with the Holy-Spirit awareness that God has provided healing.

A stranger to this earth, God's Remnant is keenly aware that all circumstances need alert eyes and ears. The pilgrim is aware that wise choices must be made. The stranger on this earth, God's child, does not feel quite at home with the customs and lifestyles in an unfamiliar area. The stranger is also looked upon as someone a bit different, and the difference is Jesus.

The Remnant believer lives to glorify God through willing obedience to His moral law. *"So whether you eat or drink or whatever you do, do it all for the glory of God"* (1 Corinthians 10:31).

Today!

Choosing to live as a Remnant of God is the best choice you will ever make. What is in your life today that prevents you from living in the Promised Land? Has God brought you to this book so you might recognize that you have a choice to cross the river from the desert to the land of His provision and be His Remnant love? His promises are available to you. This is the only reality in the crumbling social and personal structure of this present day. There must be some anchor in your life besides yourself.

Do you feel lost, lonely, or confused today? Are the struggles of your life overwhelming you? The forces of darkness rejoice, because they hate God and want to hurt Him. God yearns to love and comfort you. Paul wrote the following to the people of Corinth: *"Praise be to the God and Father of our Lord Jesus Christ, the Father of compassion and the God of all comfort, who comforts us in all our troubles"* (2 Corinthians 1:3–4). The Father will comfort you in all of your troubles.

Is there any one of us who has not spent part of our lives in days of trouble? Have you experienced anxiety and panic over finances, success, persecution, or illness? Perhaps you've suffered the loss of a loved one—a death of one who has touched your life. In all your troubles, the canopy of comfort will cover you, if your heart is simply surrendered through Christ.

I have heard the cries of many people bitterly complaining that God has not heard their prayers, or that God is never of any help. These calls often sound more like a demand, not a cry. For example, a young woman I know, whom I will call Jane (not her name) was in the midst of divorcing her husband. She admitted that she had been regularly involved in sexual affairs and lies. Her need, as she stated, was for God to solve her problems with both her husband and their finances. Yet she was totally unwilling to learn about God's Word, His character, and His call for her heart to change.

As her life was disintegrating around her, I understood that the self-willed life of her earthly father had well-trained this woman to seek pleasure as the moment brought it. She had hardened her heart toward God, just as he did. Jane was seeking any momentary escape from day-to-day responsibility. This is a young woman who remains in my prayers. I know without a shadow of a doubt there is great tragedy ahead for her. She is repeating the generational sin of leading her young daughter to spiritual death.

Her choice of moral code was a learned legacy from her earthly father, who modeled to his daughters that immorality was acceptable. His own satisfactions often came before moral training and the well-being of his children. Spiritual training was non-existent.

Unusual? No, again and again this is repeated by men and women from every area of the world. They refuse to accept the life truth that requires a parent to be accountable to God. Generation after generation misses God's offer and God's power to turn a heart toward Him.

God gives each individual a choice, but remember, God is God! We must not try to mold Him like a piece of silly putty to become what we would like Him to be. He is God, the Creator, and is holy in all He does. Each individual, including Jane, must personally accept or reject the God of Abraham, Isaac and Jacob.

One day, Jane will recall the offers from God to draw her into the life of promise. She will remember those who shared Christ with her. Jane will tumble into the future with her mind screaming, because she will never be satisfied. Her attempted manipulations will not succeed. She will see herself through a mirror of shadows of dark forces and not as a woman made in the image of God.

What about the father who was entrusted to teach his little girl about her security as a child of God? Who was called to model God Himself to the growing teen? This parent was supposed to leave a legacy of love, faith, mercy, and, most of all, truth. The gift of this child who was given to him by the great Lord God was not honored.

This parent has left a legacy of self-centered, unhappy children. Each of his children has failed in interpersonal relationships. They have never known that God is not the same as their faithless father.

I am not sure if Jane's father will seek the truth before the end of his life. If not, how tragic that day will be. He will discover that everything he pursued was meaningless and vanishes in a heartbeat. He will have left a trash dump behind instead of a golden treasure.

Present and Powerful

Drawing close to God begins with calling out to the Father for His presence to surround you. He is there. His attributes include being omnipresent and omnipotent.

Omnipresent? What is that? God alone has this attribute. God is free of the limitations of time and space. His power, intelligence, and goodness embrace and penetrate all His work.[14]

Beloved reader, this means that if you picture God as distant, limited, or as a carved idol, consider again. God is not defined by time and space as you know it. This is why prayer and the Word are essential to your very life. His presence is everywhere. He is not a table, a piece of wood, a star, a moon, a sun, or a human. He is God, omnipresent in the midst of all His created works:

"Can anyone hide in secret places so that I cannot see him?" declares the Lord. "Do not I fill heaven and earth?" declares the Lord. (Jeremiah 23:24)

Another exclusive attribute of God is His absolute power, His omnipotence. He is able to do everything that is in harmony with His wise, holy, and perfect nature.[15]

Beloved reader, there is a peaceful rest in God for the Remnant. He is all powerful. The Remnant may face difficult circumstances, but God will not be defeated by those circumstances. God will never be defeated.

Create no other gods for yourself. Be alert to the dangers of denying the reality of who God is. He clearly defines Himself in His Word. The Lord God says, *"I am God Almighty"* (Genesis 17:1).

Notes

1. P. Meier, *Bruised and Broken* (Grand Rapids: Baker Book House, 1993), p. 207.

2. Anonymous.

3. Randy Alcorn, *Eternal Perspectives* (July/August 1994).

4. Jacquelyn Buerstatte, 1996. Used with permission.

5. M. Unger, *Unger's Bible Dictionary* (Chicago: Moody Press, 1966), p. 511.

6. Ibid.

7. Ibid., p. 512.

8. P. D. Fritz, *Living as a Trustworthy Woman of God* (Reno, NV: Crowne Emerald Publishers, 1996), p. 136.

9. C. Simcox, *3000 Quotations on Christian Themes* (Grand Rapids: Baker Book House, 1989), p. 68.

10. Ibid.

11. Hearst Corporation, "1996 AMA Report: TV Mayhem Stirs Kids' Violence," *San Francisco Examiner* (10 September 1996): p. 1.

12. J. Havemann, *Washington Post* (reprinted in *Reno Gazette Journal,* 7 February 1997, p. 1).

13. Ibid.

14. Unger, *Unger's Bible Dictionary,* p. 809.

15. Ibid., p. 808.

Chapter 3

The Gatherings

The New Testament book of Acts records the history of the early Christians, referred to as the Church, in the period after the death and resurrection of God the Son, Jesus Christ. The book of Acts, chapter seven, provides a spiritual history of the people of Israel. This spiritual history began in the Garden of Eden. Let's take a journey through this history by examining several special lives. We will discover that God always gathers His beloved to Himself.

The spiritual lifeline of God's people can be seen through the lives of Abraham, Joseph, Moses, the prophets, and others. These were Remnant people. There are many people throughout history who walked with God. By looking at several who chose to listen, believe, and live faithfully, you and I can begin to understand Remnant people.

Abraham

God chose Abraham to establish His people. Abraham did not know this, but he obeyed the voice of Lord to simply go wherever the Lord God called him. Born in 2166 B.C., Abraham was called from Ur to the land of Canaan, where he died in 1991 B.C. He was declared righteous by faith (Genesis 15:6). The God of glory appeared to Abraham and said, *"Leave...go...I will show you"* (Genesis 12:1). Abraham obeyed.

Abraham is the father of Israel and the father of the Remnant believer today as well. Trustworthy God desires that you trust Him as a Remnant believer today. God described Himself in Exodus 3:15:

> *Say to the Israelites, "The Lord, the God of your fathers— the God of Abraham, the God of Isaac and the God of Jacob—has sent me to you." This is My name forever, the name by which I am to be remembered from generation to generation.*

Abraham was called a servant of God. God described him to Abraham's son Isaac, *"I am the God of your father Abraham. Do not be afraid, for I am with you; I will bless you and will increase the number of your descendants for the sake of My servant Abraham"* (Genesis 26:24).

This is spoken by God the Father to you as the Remnant today. *"Do not be afraid, for I am with you,"* your deeply intimate God says. Have you faced fear today—fears about your job, your finances, your husband or wife, your children, your safety, or your personal worth? God Almighty promises that He is *"with you"*! I can assure you, it is a fact that your outlook, confidence, and security will experience a powerful change when you face a fearful situation by speaking aloud the commitment of Genesis 26:24.

I will bless you, _____. Do not be

(write your name)

afraid, for I am with you.

54

A power-filled and secure life is given to the servant of God. As a servant of God, you are also His friend. God has a special plan and promise for every Remnant believer. He delights in delighting us. Like a great artist and true friend, He has designed what is the very best for you. You decide to choose a pilgrimage with Him and for Him.

I want to be called a servant of God and then, like Abraham, to be called a friend of God. Do you ever feel alone, or have friends ever failed you? Lift your eyes to your Friend, the Lord God Almighty. Know the character of your Friend as described by King Jehoshaphat of Judah during 872–848 B.C.:

> *O Lord, God of our fathers, are You not the God who is in heaven? You rule over all the kingdoms of the nations. Power and might are in Your hand, and no one can withstand You. O our God, did You not drive out the inhabitants of this land before Your people Israel and give it forever to the descendants of Abraham Your friend?*
>
> (2 Chronicles 20:6–7)

James, a disciple of Christ, wrote to the twelve tribes, who were scattered among the nations around the year A.D. 60: "*And the scripture was fulfilled that says, 'Abraham believed God, and it was credited to him as righteousness,' and he was called God's friend*" (James 2:23).

What comes to your mind about having or being a friend? Commitment, respect, intimacy, trustworthiness, and compassion are aspects of the relationship between friends. Note that James tells us righteousness was credited to Abraham because Abraham believed God. Abraham, as recorded in the book of Genesis, was very much a human being. He fell short of God's glory time and again. However, this man was a great hero of our faith. Abraham learned, as you and I do, through joys, trials, successes, and struggles.

Abraham did not simply say, "Okay, I believe You, God." But God, who knows our hearts, knew that Abraham believed Him because he believed *in* God! The Remnant believes God for every promise and believes that God's moral laws must be obeyed. In doing so, the Remnant will have the pleasure, joy, and peace of friendship with God.

Friendship is a marvelous aspect of the Remnant's radiant relationship with God. The God of Abraham is the same God today. He knows you as intimately as he did Abraham, whom He called into being both His servant and friend.

God called Abraham to make a personal pilgrimage with Him. Abraham listened to God, who made seven promises to him in Genesis 12:1–3:

1. I will make you a great nation.
2. I will bless you.
3. I will make your name great.
4. You will be a blessing.
5. I will bless those who bless you.
6. Whoever curses you I will curse.
7. All people on earth will be blessed through you.

The covenants God made with Abraham are recorded in Genesis 12:1–3. God also made the following covenant with Abraham:

I am God Almighty; walk before Me and be blameless. I will confirm My covenant between Me and you and will greatly increase your numbers....You will be the father of many nations....The whole land of Canaan, where you are now an alien, I will give as an everlasting possession to you and your descendants after you; and I will be their God. (Genesis 17:1–2, 4, 8)

You can understand the heart of God for us through His relationship with Abraham. God offers the same relationship to the faithful Remnant as the one He established with Abraham. God will keep His promise to keep and to gather faithful people.

Remember, a Remnant believer is one who has a heart relationship with God. A believer makes the decision to surrender every detail of his life to the will of God. A believer trusts God to determine what is best for him. A believer places God first.

Abraham had a heart to trust God and to be righteous. On his pilgrimage, he made slips and detours, but God led his journey. God's grace preserved Abraham and his descendants and preserves the Remnant believer to this day.

Reading the Bible breathes truth and life into you. The most read book of all time contains the standards, warnings, blessings, and promises of God to you for this very moment in time. You need not live in confusion or disillusionment.

Abraham honored his covenant with God and waited faithfully for many, many years for a descendant, even though both he and his wife Sarah were very old. Most have heard of the miracle birth of Isaac to an aging Sarah (Genesis 21).

The Scriptures in the book of Genesis describe the lives of Abraham and Sarah. God has left you and me an incredible witness. His Word can be trusted completely. He does what He says He will do. A relationship between God and a Remnant believer is built by trusting God. Even though you may stumble along and sometimes make decisions on your own about how God should keep the promise, He will refine your life as He works out His promises to you. Abraham and Sarah had to have faith to believe beyond naturally defined possibilities. You, as a child of God, can know your God will also bring about the best in your life. Obedient and faithful hearts can rest in God.

Joseph

But God was with him and rescued him from all his trou-
bles. (Acts 7:9–10)

Through Abraham and Sarah's son Isaac, the line of God's promise (Genesis 17:2) continued through Jacob, whose twelve sons became the Patriarchs, heads of the twelve tribes of Israel.

One of the sons, Joseph, was dearly loved by his father. Joseph's jealous brothers forced him to become a slave in Egypt. A man of honor, he was cast into prison due to false accusation. He was forgotten and forlorn it would seem. Perhaps you have experienced a great injustice in your own life. Perhaps you have tried to follow God and have felt abandoned by Him. Joseph surely felt deep hurt as the result of his brothers' betrayal. Joseph was first a slave and then a prisoner, but God protected him. Certainly a victim of human greed, he suffered, because he chose to be a man of integrity, a Remnant man.

The account of Joseph's pilgrimage is found in Genesis 37 and 39–50. This Remnant man remained faithful to the God he knew and loved. God gave Joseph, a covenant man, the strength to endure. He could be trusted to rescue Abraham's line, God's people, from famine and extinction. By the time God's people went to live in Egypt, God had made Joseph a powerful leader. They returned to the Promised Land 400 years later, just as God had promised.

Moses

Close to 400 years after Joseph, the group of God's people who went to Egypt had survived but had become slaves of the Egyptians. They were both oppressed and abused. The people cried out to God for deliverance:

The Israelites groaned in their slavery and cried out, and their cry for help because of their slavery went up to God. God heard their groaning and He remembered His covenant with Abraham, with Isaac and with Jacob.

(Exodus 2:23–24)

God prepared a man called Moses (1526–1406 B.C.) to deliver the Israelites. God provided a miraculous rescue of baby Moses by Pharaoh's daughter. Moses was then raised in royal robes as the Pharaoh's son. As an adult he was forced into exile and lived as a fugitive. After 40 desert years, a plan was to unfold for history to record (Exodus 3–4).

Moses had once attempted to protect God's people in Egypt and had been scorned, threatened, and rejected. Although Moses escaped to the desert, no doubt in much fear, God's shield had been around him since birth. God knew His plan for Moses, and now it was time to call him from shepherding the flock of sheep to shepherding the flock of God. If you are a yielded Remnant believer, God is preparing you according to His plan. The life of Moses is not just good story material. We have a record of it so we can understand God and how He works through us.

In exile, Moses became separated from his biological family as well as the royal Egyptian family who had raised him. When God is preparing us according to His plan, we are sometimes in isolated, desert experiences as well. Often, God wants your undivided attention. Moses tended his father-in-law's flock in the Midian Desert. He felt the desolation of the desert, but certainly he had the shepherd's deep care and concern for the flock of sheep in his care. He went to the far side of the desert and came to Horeb, the mountain of God, and the burning bush. Can you picture the man, Moses, when out of that bush, he heard:

Moses! Moses!...I am the God of your father, the God of Abraham, the God of Isaac and the God of Jacob.

(Exodus 3:4, 6)

Six hundred years earlier, God had promised Abraham He would preserve generations. He preserved His people through Joseph in Egypt and now would preserve them through His servant Moses. The timing is always up to God Himself. God's promise to His covenant people rings out as God says:

> *I have indeed seen the misery of My people in Egypt. I have heard them crying out because of their slave drivers, and I am concerned about their suffering. So I have come down to rescue them from the hand of the Egyptians and to bring them up out of that land into a good and spacious land.*
>
> (Exodus 3:7–8)

Remember that a covenant relationship with God promises His great blessings, but in return, the Remnant believer's promise must be obedience and faith:

> *Now if you obey Me fully and keep My covenant, then out of all nations you will be My treasured possession.*
>
> (Exodus 19:5)

A treasured possession is a people belonging to God. Both the individual and the body of Christians today are to be set apart and are to do His will:

> *For you are a people holy to the Lord your God.*
>
> (Deuteronomy 7:6)

> *You are a people holy to the Lord your God.*
>
> (Deuteronomy 14:2, 21)

A heart can belong to the world, the flesh, and the enemy. It is possible to create a golden calf of your religious performance by memorizing all the Scriptures so that you can prove yourself right in correcting others. Nothing reeks of self more than a false superiority of religious knowledge. The Word should be in your memory so it can be within your heart. That golden calf may deceptively glow brightly to the arrogant mind, but God is not found there. Nor was He found in the frenzied laughter of Satan when the Israelites refused to believe God.

As they waited for the return of Moses from meeting with God on Mount Sinai, Exodus 32 tells us they gathered together to defy God. Consider the behavior of the Israelites when God and Moses seemed to be out of sight. Moses had been called by God to deliver His Covenant to those He had delivered out of slavery:

> *Come, make us gods who will go before us. As for this fellow Moses who brought us up out of Egypt, we don't know what has happened to him.* (Exodus 32:1)

Waiting in the desert was not for the Israelites. They demanded a calf idol of gold that would make them secure in the desert. No way would they wait for Moses to descend from his meeting with God on Mount Sinai. The people cried out that they had chosen to trust the false god of their Egyptian slaveholders.

Satan and his demonic host must howl in delight to this day. It was so easy to tempt a gathering of the Remnant. They had come out of Egypt and across the Red Sea. Now they had turned into a crowd that gathered to make their own god. How Satan's camp must have laughed at the fury of the Remnant man, Moses, and at the anger of God, who saw the dark celebration of the Israelites around their newly-made calf idol.

No doubt the fires of hell itself burned more brightly at the prospect of future welcome guests. At the altar of the calf idol, the people said that this was the god that delivered them from Egypt (Exodus 32:4). This was the defiance of a people who declared their own festival at the beginning of a new day. They rose to sacrifice to their own god and made offerings to the calf idol. That done, they sought to pleasure themselves in food, drink, and immorality. Brighter, brighter the flames of hell burned to the delight of the enemy. The depravity of their celebrations seemed as fun and as pleasurable as the free-for-all lifestyles throughout the nations today.

Was this action so far apart from many ways in our lives now? What do you choose to worship as you rise each morning? Is it the true and mighty God? Do you go to His altar and worship early before any decisions are made? Have you experienced the great joy of being alone with God before anything else distracts your heart and your soul?

Time and again I have heard from hurting people who claim they did ask God, and He did not answer. Many times I have heard this from those who have made their own golden calf to worship. From a woman, it could be a relationship that she thought would make her happy. From a man, it could be a possession or a success. From both, I did not hear that they were willing to love the Lord with all their hearts, all their souls, and all their minds (Matthew 22:37). Over and over again, God has been asked to give favors to the self-willed idol worshipper.

We sometimes carefully construct calf idols. We choose to make them from what is important to us. For example, this could be the house-proud woman who continually scolds her children if a mark is left on a piece of furniture. Her house is her idol for others to come and see that she has material goods. A calf idol could be a man's portfolio of stocks or a business title that makes him feel he is worthwhile. It could also be abuse, anger, and control. Jealousy is a calf idol that develops in a mind that does not accept God's ownership of the world. It is God's sovereign right to determine the best life plan for each person.

Although God has open arms of forgiveness for a heart that is broken before Him and is ready to change direction, He is not pleased when an occasional request or acknowledgment is tossed His way. The consequences of our building calf idols may seem far off when we busily allow the idols to have first altar space in our lives. The consequences, however, will come. The consequence can often be that we are allowed to bow to the calf idol for years. A wasted life is a dreadful consequence.

The community of Christians can be the worst offenders of God's heart. Today they continue to act as the Israelites, often smug and often apathetic. Through the centuries, God's reaction should have been remembered. He was angered by unfaithful people. His reaction was spoken to Moses:

> *Go down, because your people, whom you brought up out of Egypt, have become corrupt. They have been quick to turn away from what I commanded them and have made themselves an idol cast in the shape of a calf. They have bowed down to it and sacrificed to it and have said, "These are your gods, O Israel, who brought you up out of Egypt." I have seen these people...and they are a stiff-necked people. Now leave Me alone so that My anger may burn against them....Then I will make you into a great nation.*
> (Exodus 32:7–10)

Oh no! Was the covenant with Abraham about to be severed by God? No. God knew He would keep His promise to His Remnant man. Moses was being equipped in the presence of Almighty God, who would prepare and equip the Remnant people for the coming forty years. Moses pleaded with God, and God relented, sending Moses and the Remnant man Joshua to the lower ground where evil was being celebrated.

There were consequences, and they were severe. God is Almighty, and He demands a righteous people. The Israelites' unbelief brought a plague upon them (Exodus 32:35). Their unfaithfulness led them to rebellion when they refused to cross into the Promised Land after they first reached the Jordan (Numbers 14:33–34).

And so the rebellious people wandered in the desert for forty years. They had brought upon themselves a delay in crossing to the Promised Land. A whole generation of calf idol worshippers and God-defying people would be dead. They would not gather at the Jordan River, and they would not enter the Land of Promise. We can so easily open a door and welcome the deceiver into our lives.

Gathered at the Jordan

The Israelites' spiritual history and their spiritual future was to be carefully recorded so you would know God's *faithfulness*. It also enables you to recognize the same *faithlessness* in people today.

Almighty God is the God of deliverance and covenant relationship to His Remnant—the people of His heart. In the fortieth year and eleventh month after crossing the Red Sea, a new crossing was about to take place. The hour had come and the command of God was given, *"Go in and take possession of the land that the Lord swore He would give to your fathers—to Abraham, Isaac and Jacob—and to their descendants after them"* (Deuteronomy 1:8). God's heart will bless you, as He blessed Abraham's descendants, in His promise.

Forty years after the Red Sea crossing, the Israelites were gathered at the shores of the Jordan. They were about to cross to the Promised Land and were excited, but possibly fearful of the unknown. They had been prepared by the cleansing years of desert wandering and the clarity of God's directions through Moses. The book of Deuteronomy is a record of God's careful equipping of His Remnant. Many would be remembering the accounts of their fathers and mothers, uncles, aunts, and members of the twelve tribes of Israel. How many were recalling the faint hearts of the past generation who had miraculously walked through a dry Red Sea? They remembered the golden calf that had been made from the items God had provided for their needs as they fled from Egypt. It is hard to believe that some of this generation, about to enter new life at last, would possibly cross the Jordan carrying an idol or false fear in their hearts.

This was the Remnant, a gathering of people ready to receive a life designed before creation. They had been taught personally by God and had witnessed both the wrath and blessings of Almighty God.

"Hear, O Israel!" (Deuteronomy 6:4). Hear, O Remnant of God, My beloved people who are to cross into possession and receive the promises I have made to you. This is His cry from the heavenly throne today, a cry that should be heard throughout the world. We must hear the Word of God as given to us through the Scripture. Hear and live!

What does God our Father tell us to hear? He wants us to listen to Him and eat His Word as bread so the decrees and laws He gave us through Moses become our food. Why? So as His people, we may live and may go in and take possession of the land (Deuteronomy 4:1–2).

> *The land you are entering to take over is not like the land of Egypt, from which you have come, where you planted your seed and irrigated it by foot as in a vegetable garden. But the land you are crossing the Jordan to take possession of is a land of mountains and valleys that drinks rain from heaven. It is a land the Lord your God cares for; the eyes of the Lord your God are continually on it from the beginning of the year to its end.* (Deuteronomy 11:10–12)

Before you read further, this would be a good time to stand at your Jordan River, looking across to the promises of God. Many times you may have felt that you also were wandering, perhaps lost, in a scorching desert. At those times you may even have called to God to help you, to heal you, or to provide for you. What we learn from the experiences of the Israelites is that God is God. He has designed the way of life and commands us to walk on His path. We must search our heart condition and trust God. If you are faithful, God is faithful.

In every life, there is a moment in time when one stands at the water's edge and is given the opportunity to walk across the river to live on the other side. God's pure and holy love created and chose to have a special people, who would in return choose to walk in love relationship with Him. What a wonderful fact that is! Surely one could not desire more than that during an earthly existence.

Ready to Cross

Excited, eager, nervous, and anxious, the Israelites were poised on the banks of the Jordan ready to cross to the other side. They and the previous generation had experienced God's love deeply. They had seen His miracles and heard His voice through Moses.

The questions and choices you are facing today, and all that your family, culture, and nation face, are not really different from the questions faced by the men and women gathered at the Jordan River. They had received God's clear instructions from Moses for His blessing of a prosperous future in the Promised Land. Prepared by God to face the battles of life ahead, they still were pilgrims on a journey to His forever kingdom. The Remnant was chosen for His service and His glory. Their purpose was to live in righteousness so the world would know He is the Lord God.

Carefully follow and pay attention to what God told the Israelites. Picture them, poised to cross the waters of the Jordan. They had personally heard His promises and had agreed to keep their covenant promise to God. Now, they were crossing to possess the land, and they were commanded to fear God, to walk in all His ways, to love Him, and to serve Him (Deuteronomy 10:12). No doubt, they were saying, "Yes! Yes! I will! I want to possess the Promised Land!"

For some, the stern warning of God was imprinted on their minds and hearts as they looked out to the new horizons:

> *Do not turn aside from any of the commands I give you today, to the right or to the left, following other gods and serving them.* (Deuteronomy 28:14)

They knew the past generation had invoked His wrath, and they remembered the results. God dealt with the rebellious people who refused to trust Him and those who worshipped the calf idol of Egypt at Mount Sinai. They endured the forty-year desert wandering. A generation died and missed the Promised Land. Yes, now they remembered His mighty hand of deliverance at the Red Sea. They had turned unfaithfully to the left and right. God had gathered His people and carried them to a new land, but they had turned their hearts back to Egypt and slavery.

Would He bless those remaining if they, too, turned to the right or left? The warnings were very clear, with no room for doubt that God's commands must be honored. He said:

> *However, if you do not obey the Lord your God and do not carefully follow all His commands and decrees I am giving you today, all these curses will come upon you and overtake you.* (Deuteronomy 28:15)

Gathered at the Jordan, and ready to cross, they were prepared to receive the promises of God. The Promised Land would be theirs at last. There was opportunity once again to live as God's Remnant. They would surely face battles. Since Adam and

Eve left the Garden of Eden, unrighteousness prowled the earth. But God would be with them. He had given them the plans, an architect's blueprint written on their hearts. God gave them the option of blessings or curses.

Almighty God, who had preserved for Himself a Remnant who would be faithful in heart relationship with Him, spoke with both love and authority:

> *Now what I am commanding you today is not too difficult for you or beyond your reach. It is not up in heaven, so that you have to ask, "Who will ascend into heaven to get it and proclaim it to us so we may obey it?" Nor is it beyond the sea, so that you have to ask, "Who will cross the sea to get it and proclaim it to us so we may obey it?" No, the word is very near you; it is in your mouth and in your heart so you may obey it. See, I set before you today life and prosperity, death and destruction. For I command you today to love the Lord your God, to walk in His ways, and to keep His commands, decrees and laws; then you will live and increase, and the Lord your God will bless you in the land you are entering to possess. But if your heart turns away and you are not obedient, and if you are drawn away to bow down to other gods and worship them, I declare to you this day that you will certainly be destroyed. You will not live long in the land you are crossing the Jordan to enter and possess. This day I call heaven and earth as witnesses against you that I have set before you life and death, and blessings and curses. Now choose life, so that you and your children may live and that you may love the Lord your God, listen to His voice, and hold fast to Him. For the Lord is your life, and He will give you many years in the land He swore to give to your fathers, Abraham, Isaac and Jacob.* (Deuteronomy 30:11–20)

Each person who was ready to cross the Jordan had heard His Word; each had the blueprint of life. Each had heard the experiences of family and friends as they were brought out of slavery. Each mother, father and child knew that Moses was God's messenger, and each knew of the powerful meeting on Mount Sinai. Each knew His message. Each had God's wrath at the hearts that had turned back to Egypt imprinted on their minds. Each knew the results of 1) building the calf idol of gold and 2) defying God by not trusting Him.

They waited forty years, enduring the consequences of that generation. God's faithfulness to His promise and His refinement of His beloved had brought them to the Jordan River. They were about to leave the old life behind. They could sing the song God instructed Moses to teach the gathered assembly, a song of the history of the people and the faithfulness of God:

> *Let My teaching fall like rain and My words descend like*
> *dew.*   (Deuteronomy 32:2)

God's hand had written on their hearts the knowledge that He alone is God, and that He alone had carried them to the river. They were to sing His Word as a song to remind themselves of the power of God. They were to sing His song of instruction to their children so the next generation would know Him. They were to be a Remnant people, according to Deuteronomy 32:1–43.

> *When Moses finished reciting all these words to all Israel,*
> *he said to them, "Take to heart all the words I have sol-*
> *emnly declared to you this day, so that you may command*
> *your children to obey carefully all the words of this law.*
> *They are not just idle words for you—they are your life. By*
> *them you will live long in the land you are crossing the*
> *Jordan to possess."*   (Deuteronomy 32:45–47)

God had given His moral law to them, both as a people and individually. He was their God. His presence and His words to them have shown you as well that God is always present in all we do. Who has offered you such a relationship? Consider who He is:

> *The Lord reigns, He is robed in majesty; the Lord is robed in majesty and is armed with strength....Your throne was established long ago; you are from all eternity....Your statutes stand firm; holiness adorns your house for endless days, O Lord.* (Psalm 93:1, 2, 5)

His words are life, as God told His beloved people. God had purified them. They were a new generation with new life, corrected by God so they would know He alone was God. Now they were ready, living in trust and in power relationship with Him and about to receive the Promised Land. Are you willing to cross now? Do you trust the promises of God? Have you seen the results deep within yourself of remaining in a desert?

As you stand at your Jordan River, the Father still welcomes you into a Remnant life. He still demands we take His words to heart and obey them. The Remnant has a heart turned to God. The Remnant has a heart for obedience before all else. If you wish to cross your Jordan River, you can choose life in the Promised Land. You can choose blessings or curses. Ritualistic practices are not the way to an intimate relationship with your Father. You may go directly to Him right now and ask Him to be the strength in your life, acknowledging His majesty and holiness.

I know that I myself am growing toward completion. I know the truth is that God the Holy Spirit will take my heart and turn it toward the ways of God. He hears my heart cry to Him alone, and He will hear yours. He knows I have chosen to live for Him.

Imagine living in the Promised Land as God's Remnant, living set apart and filled with purpose. He knows of all your failings and offers forgiveness to your repentant heart. A life for you under His shield is waiting.

Believe God for your moment-by-moment life. Stop pleasing man and please God alone. He will go before you and walk with you as your strength. *"'Because he loves me,' says the Lord, 'I will rescue him'"* (Psalm 91:14). Do you truly love God? You must know Him to love Him. You cannot be in loving relationship without deep knowledge of the One you love.

Trust Him to welcome you as a child of His promise. You will live as a stranger to those who do not love Him through Christ. But God is no stranger to those whose hearts are turned toward Him. As a child of the promise, you will receive a heart of peace, confidence, and security.

The Israelites at the Jordan may have had the same questions you might have at the moment you choose to cross your Jordan River to His Remnant life. Do you wonder if Remnant life in the Promised Land will bring you security or fortune? Are you afraid of new territory? Are you afraid of those who will oppose you because you worship your God only?

These could have been the thoughts of the men and women looking across the Jordan. They no longer had Moses to lead them. Moses had been taken to his home with the Lord God; his work had been completed. The joy of the eternal Promised Land with the Father was his at last. Now, God appointed a faithful warrior, Joshua, who would be entrusted to shepherd them. Would the Israelites trust God under the new leadership of Joshua?

Perhaps many were not only eager to leave the barren desert behind, and looked forward to the green, productive land across the river, but wondered if it was to be all that God had promised. Actually, some of the Israelites may have already been thinking that the desert wasn't so bad. Hadn't God given them food to eat and been close to them in the desert? So what if there were few trees for shade and scarce water for their thirst in the barren land? They had survived, so why not stay comfortable? No doubt there were many who felt that God really had given them too big a challenge. They had, however, made a covenant with God.

The Jordan River, to begin with, was at flood stage. How could these gathered people cross the river safely? Was God kidding? Is He kidding you with His promises? They had probably not learned to swim, and the Promised Land was across all that water. What does your Jordan River look like to you today? Could the Promised Land be available only to the strong navigators of life and not to you?

After all, would God ask you to cross a flood-stage river? Perhaps it would be best to stay just where you are. As a comfortable believer in God, you really don't need to be a strong swimmer or a leader or a warrior. Maybe you could remain a desert dweller who prefers to make your own way.

In the midst of God's desire to deliver you from a barren life, you could actually hold onto the old with fierce arms. This could be especially true if you do not have faith and trust in God today through His Word and prayer. Ask the Holy Spirit to fill you with the ability to trust God. Triumphant life comes from your prayer and stillness before the Lord. Stand poised at the river, allowing the Holy Spirit to gently, yet assuredly, give you understanding. Faith empowers your first step.

God gives His chosen leaders directions and does speak through them, but your eyes should not look to a person. Seek God in His Word and prayer. All that is done in a Remnant believer's life should be out of love for God and for the glory of God.

The Remnant is not shaken by the failings of man. The Remnant believer has personal knowledge of God's faithfulness. Receiving life's blueprint from the Lord God through His Word and through communication with Him is as natural as breath itself.

Who is the God of Israel? What has He said to us as we face a decision to cross to His promises and to become a Remnant believer? Gathered Israelites were reminded who He was as Moses blessed the tribes:

> *There is no one like the God of Jeshurun, who rides on the heavens to help you and on the clouds in His majesty. The eternal God is your refuge, and underneath are the everlasting arms. He will drive out your enemy before you, saying, "Destroy him!" So Israel will live in safety alone; Jacob's spring is secure in a land of grain and new wine, where the heavens drop dew. Blessed are you, O Israel! Who is like you, a people saved by the Lord? He is your shield and helper and your glorious sword.*
>
> (Deuteronomy 33:26–29)

This is God who speaks today to you as a covenant believer. Why would you depend upon yourself when you have such a powerful source of life?

Each one of us must look deeply within ourselves to answer that question. There are always rivers to cross and mountains in our way, because we live in this imperfect world. This world is filled with those who hate God and oppose you. But remember, He is your shield, helper and glorious sword.

Judges and Kings

Consider the reminder of the sovereignty of God and His power: "I brought you out of slavery." This is a love statement. It is a proclamation of freedom for those who know God and are obedient to Him. Loyalty, meaning loving obedience, means you can be free.

After crossing the Jordan, it was not long before rebellion and disobedience reigned in the Promised Land. God had once placed those He loved in the Garden, and they rebelled. In His faithfulness and mercy, He once again placed them in a Land of Promise. God required that they live according to His ways, because His ways were life. The women and men of the promise turned their hearts to surroundings and circumstances once again. It appears that when His people lived in provision and protection, they rebelled and made surroundings and self objects of worship.

God did not sit by and quietly watch the growing idol worship or the assimilation of the cults and cultures into His appointed ones' lives. He warned them time and again through the holy prophets. He allowed trials and devastation in their land so they would turn back to Him. Always, He gave them a choice; always, He left open the door of repentance; always, He kept His part of His covenant.

The ancient cry of Deuteronomy is heard throughout the ages and in our churches today, "Hear, O Israel." The time lines may be different, but once again, people and leaders remain the same. Is not God even more magnificent in His mercy when we look back at the depth and extent of His forgiveness over thousands of years? How precious are the believers who stand before Him today, the links of gold in the Remnant chain, living in triumph.

"Give us a king!" The people living in the Promised Land wanted to replace God's plan of government. What had happened to those gathered at the Jordan? The descendants of the people who had walked across the Jordan into the Promised Land were now rejecting God's plan. These were people with whom God had made a covenant and people who had entered into this covenant relationship. This Remnant had been delivered from the harsh slavery of the land of Egypt.

The Promised Land had been entered. The people had served the Lord under the faithful leadership of the successor of Moses. God had appointed the warrior Joshua, who had led them in the way of the Lord. What happened after the death of Joshua? The people breached the covenant and incited God's anger.

God's ideal plan for His people was that Moses, Joshua, and then generations of judges would lead Israel. They were to tend to His people, who were to obey God. Thus the people would live as a Remnant people in covenant relationship, obeying and receiving His promises.

Now, about 325 years later, the leaders of Israel demanded a king. In response to the demands of the people, God allowed them to choose to have a king. This changed the rule of Israel from a God-led theocracy to a man-led people. They failed to believe that the way of the omniscient God is the best for His creation. Rebellion leads to a ruptured society. Restoration would come only from a future King, the Redeemer. He came 2,000 years ago and rules today.

When the people were about to cross the Jordan, Moses was told by God that this rebellion would occur. Thus, Moses gave the Israelites God's specific qualifications for a king. Deuteronomy 17:14–20 includes these qualifications; among these were that the king must submit to God. The king was not above God's law and must not *"consider himself better than his brothers."* The laws that God had spoken to His people were the laws for the Promised Land:

> *When he takes the throne of his kingdom, he is to write for himself on a scroll a copy of this law, taken from that of the priests, who are Levites. It is to be with him, and he is to read it all the days of his life so that he may learn to revere the Lord his God and follow carefully all the words of*

> *this law and these decrees and not consider himself better*
> *than his brothers and turn from the law to the right or to*
> *the left.* (Deuteronomy 17:18–20)

God knew that a Remnant would always remain faithful to Him. He knew human failure as well, and He would not break His promise to the covenant keepers. Although those who refused to live His way may have thought they were acting in wisdom, the devastation of the Israelites would result from this choice.

A heart refusing the way of the sovereign God always sinks further into dark waters and is eventually overcome by those waters. The heart hardens and the mind believes in itself. God extended a choice of government by the world's system to the Israelites. They demanded what they saw in the pagan nations around them. The Israelites wanted power and wealth. God knew what would follow but still gave them the opportunity to be protected by godly kings who would lead for Him. With obedience would come a promise and an assurance of blessing:

> *Then he and his descendants will reign a long time over*
> *his kingdom in Israel.* (Deuteronomy 17:20)

The faithful people of a holy God would shrink in numbers. Reading through the Bible books of Kings and Chronicles, you will discover that the God who gave mankind free will would have His heart broken by those He loved so much. These books give more evidence that when the first of His children decided on self-will instead of His will, future generations would do the same.

Judges had governed from 1375 to 1050 B.C. During this time, God knew that many of the people had forsaken Him to serve other gods. The people of God chose to assimilate the gods of other nations into their lives and looked to the government of those nations as the ideal.

The Remnant will endure some severe hardships because of the sin of the world system and Satan, the rejector. They will suffer under the rebellious kings, and their hearts will long for the King of Kings to come for them.

The intimate, only God, who made Himself known through His guidance, provision and protection in the desert, was not enough. The Israelites designed their own god.

King David…King Josiah

Josiah and David are considered to have been two kings who obeyed God. We know historically, that just prior to each of their reigns, a king leading through pride and fear had angered God.

David and Josiah were the two kings who sought to honor God. Saul, the first king of the people of Israel, had proved to be a man who believed in himself before God. David was a young shepherd boy who believed God. David, whose heart God knew, was placed in position to lead God's beloved people. God prepared David through struggle and battle until He was ready to place David on the throne as the ruler of His United Kingdom of Judah and Israel (1010–970 B.C.).

King Saul did not obey God's commands and became a tormented man. He tried to take control of God's events, and the consequences were great. God holds us responsible for our actions. Saul disobeyed God in two ways. He committed unfaithful acts, and he failed to do right by God. Saul looked to God for selfish reasons only. The reason for Saul's punishment is found in 1 Chronicles:

> *Saul died for his disobedience to the Lord and because he had consulted a medium, and did not ask the Lord for*

guidance. So the Lord killed him and gave the kingdom to David. (1 Chronicles 10:13–14 TLB)

What does this have to do with you or me at this moment? Our stubbornness or disobedience to God's moral laws places us in Saul's shoes. Making decisions on our own, depending on self, man, psychics, mysticism, or false gods for wisdom, leads to devastating consequences. Consequences are given in God's timing.

During crises or failure, I have often seen women and men turn to God. Seeking God only when there is nowhere else to turn is dangerous. Knowing your heart, God just may refuse to answer, as he did to Saul. God is never fooled; He knows when a heart has not changed. God knows every heart's motives.

The most unlikely candidate for king of Israel at that time was a young boy tending his father's sheep in the fields. God chose David, a shepherd, one who had cared responsibly for a gathered flock. Then God prepared and trained David to become one of the good kings of Israel.

David was far removed from political life. Facing betrayal, conflict, and wars tested and matured David. Years would pass before the shepherd boy would become the shepherd king. He trusted God, and God was with Him. He became a mighty warrior who then became a priestly king. David ruled as the warrior/priest leader of God's beloved. Safe pasture was given to the people of the promise, God's own beloved, under King David.

David's reign was filled with success and failure. God's forgiveness is shown to us through the moral failures of David. David looked away from God and betrayed a woman and her husband. Bathsheba could not trust her king and perhaps was swayed into adultery by the handsome, powerful King David. For a moment in time, David forgot God. The consequences to them both were swift. David was broken before the Lord and repented. God responded to David's broken and contrite heart with discipline and healing.

The love of God keeps the doorway to His heart open. The door that David, you, and I need to choose is clear:

> *If My people, who are called by My name, will humble themselves and pray and seek My face and turn from their wicked ways, then will I hear from heaven and will forgive their sin and will heal their land.* (2 Chronicles 7:14)

The Lord chose David and the tribe of Judah to establish a line that would reign over Israel forever:

> *The Lord God will give him the throne of his father David, and he will reign over the house of Jacob forever; his kingdom will never end.* (Luke 1:32–33)

The great covenant made with David promised God's everlasting love, correction for sin, and:

> *Your house and your kingdom shall endure before Me forever; your throne shall be established forever.*
> (2 Samuel 7:16 NAS)

King David, a Remnant man, responded as each of us should to God's promises. David trusted God and responded in prayer and praise:

> *For the sake of Thy word, and according to Thine own heart, Thou hast done all this greatness to let Thy servant know. For this reason Thou art great, O Lord God; for there is none like Thee, and there is no God besides Thee.*
> (2 Samuel 7:21–22 NAS)

Almighty God kept His promise to David and to you by God the Son, Jesus Christ. Christ is the King of Kings, whose human birth made Him a descendant of David:

Therefore all the generations from Abraham to David are fourteen generations; and from David to the deportation to Babylon fourteen generations; and from the deportation to Babylon to the time of Christ fourteen generations.

(Matthew 1:17 NAS)

Near the end of David's life, he gave his son Solomon several principles to follow. David knew that God would bless his son. Solomon was to build God's holy temple. David trusted God and God's commands. He loved God and gathered his son and the leaders of Israel to hear his guidance to Solomon:

I am instructing you to search out every commandment of the Lord so that you may continue to rule this good land and leave it to your children to rule forever.

1. *Solomon, my son, get to know the God of your fathers.*
2. *Worship and serve Him with a clean heart and a willing mind.*
3. *For the Lord sees every heart and understands and knows every thought.*
4. *If you seek Him, you will find Him; but if you forsake Him, He will permanently throw you aside.*
5. *So be very careful, for the Lord has chosen you to build His holy Temple.*
6. *Be strong and do as He commands.*

(1 Chronicles 28:8–10 TLB, numerals added)

David's son had witnessed his father's greatness and his failures. Solomon had also witnessed David's relationship with God. David lived with a broken heart because he had betrayed God. Solomon saw the consequences of David's sin spill out on his family. God's correction was a hard learning experience for King David. However, God and David built Israel to God's glory.

Like Solomon, we too can benefit from knowing the struggles and victories of King David, not only for ourselves, but for our children. The parent who fails to model and share David's principles with a child has failed that child. This is a good time to reflect upon your parental responsibilities before God. You are given a charge and will be held accountable. The only treasure you can give is the treasure of understanding God and the treasure of a true life in the Lord's will.

Other kings followed David and his son King Solomon, but few others would be known as godly kings. Several other kings looked to God at some time during their reigns, but idolatry and faithlessness characterized the reigns of most kings.

Disobedience of the kings and the people resulted in the eventual division and devastation of the Promised Land. The Southern Kingdom of Judah was ruled by Manasseh during 696–642 B.C. His sins were among the worst of all the kings who led the Kingdom of Judah. His Canaanite practices were specifically forbidden by Mosaic Law. Manasseh's practices led to God's judgment of exile on the whole people. We see that people are blessed when leaders obey God's law. The responsibility of a leader is tremendous.

2 Kings 21:6 describes the practices that so angered God, including mediums, soothsayers, and sorcery—attributing God's powers to others. Leviticus 19:26 and Deuteronomy 18:10–14 clearly forbid these practices, yet they continue today. God forbids idolatry. Do not think that a relationship between God and His people is a one-way promise. Let us read on: *"If the people of Israel will only follow the instructions I gave them through Moses, I will never again expel them from this land of their fathers"* (2 Kings 21:8 TLB).

God was very clear. Covenant promises are realized in a two-way relationship. Was the Israelite response any different from much of the church today? *"But the people did not listen to the Lord, and Manasseh enticed them to do even more evil than the surrounding nations had done"* (2 Kings 21:9 TLB).

The same sinful nature that led to the first catastrophic tear in man's relationship with God was again ripping apart God's heart. The Israelite kings were *"enticed"* by evil, just as Eve and Adam had been. How thankful I am for the Remnant who endured the reign of King Manasseh and kept the covenant relationship alive for you and me today. I thank God for His history and teaching in the Word.

Then, we look to the radiant reign of King Josiah, who succeeded Manasseh's son Amon. Josiah was the last godly king of Judah before the exile to Babylon became reality.

Following in the footsteps of his ancestor King David, Josiah held back God's anger because he was obedient. Josiah began his reign at eight years old and eighteen years later, he gave orders to repair the temple. His grandfather Manasseh had not only built shrines on the high hills to heathen gods, but heathen altars were also placed in the temple of the Lord:

> *Manasseh even set up a shameful Asherah-idol* [Baal worship] *in the Temple—the very place that the Lord had spoken to David and Solomon about when he said, "I will place my name forever in this Temple, and in Jerusalem."*
> (2 Kings 21:7 TLB)

The prayers of Judah's Remnant must have been answered, because King Josiah gave the order to repair the temple. The temple had been used for heathen worship; the Book of Law must have been hidden away. God's law is never welcome to those making their own law. How many churches today use it if it manipulates the people but keep it hidden as the foundation for worship? What idol has been built in today's churches?

Should we call out today to repair the temple of God? Can a truly godly leader in a nation and/or church make a difference? God left us the story of Josiah to show us his response to obedience. Josiah turned first to the task of cleaning the temple and leading his flock of people in the Southern Kingdom. To his amazement, the Book of Law was discovered by the High Priest, Hilkiah. If we seek God, we will find Him. He does and will speak to the sincere heart.

As a Remnant, you must discern God's leader from a self-appointed leader. That is our responsibility as Remnant citizens. Always pray for the wisdom to know whom God has called to leadership. We need to make sure we keep God as Lord, and not our own satisfactions or compromises.

When Josiah listened to the reading of the Law, he fully recognized how far away from God's will the people had been led by evil kings. His reaction is described as terror and that, beloved reader, is a dramatic model of how we should react to disobedience. Josiah renewed the covenant relationship with God in the presence of the Lord and the people. God once again gathered His people together:

> *And the king stood by a pillar, and made a covenant before the Lord, to walk after the Lord, and to keep His commandments and His testimonies and His statutes with all their heart and all their soul, to perform the words of this covenant that were written in this book. And all the people stood to the covenant.* (2 Kings 23:3 KJV)

In the next chapter, we will see the history of Israel after the kings, along with our responsibility to live for the one true King.

Chapter 4

Designer God

You and I cannot have a designer God, one that we think will bow to our demands or trends in religious fashion.

While visiting in a city famous for its fashion designers, I walked by a room where a private fashion show was taking place. It appeared that it was being held for a wealthy Middle Eastern oil man and the women of his family.

I could see the regal-looking models parading before the family in an elegant hotel room. Everything had been set up for the occasion to delight the eye of the beholder. No doubt certain dresses of the well-known designer's line would soon belong to those who found them pleasing. Perhaps their old garments would be discarded because this spring the new, changed lines were the object of attention and delight.

I recall this not because it was an unacceptable event. The items were probably easily within the budget of these people. The analogy to the Western believer today is what I found significant. The appealing display of goods and the enchanted attention of those at the scene brought designer religions to my mind.

Designer religions are like these creations of man. The religion is designed with the gods of this world—easy gods that people feel comfortable worshipping. Like new garments, these designer religions comfort the followers with performance, easy living, or new trends.

Gathering the people to the desert and Jordan River was God's design. The Israelites compromised God when they began to live in the prosperity of the promise. They began to design not only their god, but their own form of worship. They chose to discard the garments of God. They wanted the latest religious fashions of the other nations.

God's system of judges was not current or good enough, they claimed. First Samuel 8:5 relates that the people came to the judge Samuel and protested over the way the present judges, Samuel's sons, were being dishonest.

A distressed Samuel went to God in prayer, and the Lord assured him that the people were not rejecting Samuel, but God Himself. The Lord said to him:

> *They have rejected Me as their king. As they have done from the day I brought them up out of Egypt until this day, forsaking Me and serving other gods, so they are doing to you. Now listen to them; but warn them solemnly and let them know what the king who will reign over them will do.*
> (1 Samuel 8:7–9)

Do you determine whom you would have govern your nation or your city by God's qualifications? God demanded specific qualifications of the king for the people of the promise to be blessed. Some of these included that the king was to be directed by the law of God and the word of the prophet. *"Samuel explained to the people the regulations of the kingship. He wrote them down on a scroll and deposited it before the Lord"* (1 Samuel 10:25).

Do you decide for God what the rules of your life should be? Have you decided that you are god enough to determine that the God of the Bible should make special adjustments to His character and codes of behavior in your case?

I hear these kinds of rationalizations from a variety of people who claim to pray, believe in God, and attend or not attend church. Most of these responses come from those who have never investigated to whom they bow down. Among the first thoughts I had after asking Jesus Christ to be my personal Savior was a desire to find out from the Word of God as much as I could about the character of God.

Seeking to discover who He said He is can be accomplished both by talking to Him and learning to listen as well. It was important to me to know whether the pastors and/or teachers I began to listen to were speaking the truth. There was no way I would give my life to an anonymous god or to one that was designed by man. Did my salvation hinge on the rules of religions? Religion *(Gr. threskia)*, as used here, refers to outward religious service.

Every Sunday, as a child, I was taken to a church where the religious leaders laid out rules. They had to be obeyed, or hell would follow. From the age I began to reason, up to the age I decided there was no God, I did not hear that Jesus Christ said, "Follow Me only." I heard, "Follow this church or you are wrong."

Others within this same denomination may have truly found Jesus and come to know Him. I wondered what would happen if there would be a gathering of all believers on a future day in the heavenly realm, and whether God would separate them according to man's format.

For me, the rejection of any other Christian form of worship was not in the character of the God they preached. My conclusion after many years was that these foundation stones were faulty.

If this God is God, could man dare to interpret or determine the salvation of others? Could a man-made church stand between God and His child? Why were religions rich when the poor of the world lived in sewer-filled slums? One and one did not add up to two.

Today, I know many people who know nothing more than religious interpretation. This is heartbreaking. These people seem to be filled with piety and longing for a phantom God.

Israel did not want God to be their king. The roar of the King of Kings no doubt still rings through the heavens, however, as the Lion of Judah, Jesus Christ, now prepares to come for His Remnant. This is not an issue of political parties or which candidate will be the best one. This is about the people and a nation who bow down to a false god, as lies become acceptable. A man of honor was important to America not so long ago. If it is not important to trust those we follow, we have moved into a hollow sense of greed. It's the same greed that led the Israelites, greed that seeks human power, just as our nations do today.

May God help the children of the next generation. Destruction will follow what we find acceptable as role models or heroes. Is the Christian today a role model? Ask the people around you what they have seen of Christ in the fruit of the vine called your life.

The cloud and the flame that led the Israelites' families out of slavery years ago had not been burned in their memories. The generations had forgotten the awesome sight of God personally walking with their ancestors, the Israelites, toward the miracle of the Red Sea crossing:

By day the Lord went ahead of them in a pillar of cloud to guide them on their way and by night in a pillar of fire to give them light, so that they could travel by day or night.
(Exodus 13:21)

They were never away from His presence as they made that perilous escape. After the Israelites crossed the Red Sea, God made known the very best plan of life. He chose to bless and to be in intimate relationship with a people who were to be a Remnant. A Remnant was to be set apart from the pagan nations who worshipped their own accomplishments, nature gods, and fertility gods—the designer gods of the deceived.

On Mount Sinai, God personally gave His loved ones His codes for a Remnant life. He detailed specific laws about how to live in the land of His promise. His beloved must live as godly men and women who can prosper in covenant relationship with Him. In the first five books of the Bible, God warned the chosen people, "Do not be deceived by the rebellious bowing down to the false gods of the Canaanites! Remove evil ways from your life!"

> *I am the Lord your God, who brought you out of Egypt, out of the land of slavery. You shall have no other gods before me.*   (Exodus 20:2–3)

Will you make yourself God? He will not allow that to happen. Your altars will be torn down. It may take a life of struggle, or you may think you have prospered, but He will deal with you. For a horrifying moment upon your deathbed, you may see clearly that you attempted in vain to create your own kingdom and wasted a lifetime. When is death? It is not necessarily when a person has lived to be 80 or 90 or 100 years old. Death comes to the child in the gang neighborhoods at any time. Cancer kills at any age. A group of young adults can die in a van or plane accident. The next moment may be the time for you or for me.

Have your days on earth been spent like the Tin Man in *The Wizard of Oz,* following Dorothy down the yellow brick road in search of your heart, looking for a wizard who can grant you favors? You are given a lifetime, long or short, to decide to become a set-apart love of God. There will be a moment in time when you are indeed made aware that you turned to others or things as the king of your life.

It may be a time of lost opportunities when your eyes open before the King of Kings. You will find yourself in the company of those who lived in man's kingdom and bowed down only to themselves. You will be in the company of the same Israelites who refused to love God enough to trust Him with the plans for their lives.

Then you will realize you have never sought the true home for your heart. Your heart will break in realization, like stone before a hammer blow. Jesus Christ made it clear that you are able to behold God the Father only through Jesus in the Word. No wonder the name of Jesus invokes anger and rejection in those who refuse to listen to His covenant offer.

Recently, I was sitting in a hotel lobby. An attractive couple came and sat close by me. They were nicely dressed and seemingly quite pleasant. The woman began talking to her husband while my group was in the midst of a discussion as well. I paid no attention until I heard her speak the name Jesus Christ. I paused then and realized that she was using the name as a curse. As she did, her demeanor changed. It was as though Satan himself were chortling within her.

When I hear His name used as a curse, my heart feels as though it has been slammed with a high-powered rifle shot. Jesus has been cursed since He walked the earth. Every time I hear His precious name spoken as a curse, I know that person serves the enemy. My heart is broken for that person. The man or woman calling His name this way will be shattered to recall the utterances throughout eternity unless he or she decides to bow down to His name. As Jesus Christ said:

He who rejects Me, and does not receive My sayings, has one who judges him; the word I spoke is what will judge him at the last day. (John 12:48 NAS)

God is no different today, nor has He been since the beginning of time. You are no different than those whom He delivered from the slavery and bondage of the ancient Egyptians. You and I must never make the mistake of being people who scorn God. You have the same choice to revere the holy God.

When you demand or install anything but God Almighty as a king in your life, you reject Him. If you hear His call and discover Him in the Word, you will find that you will never want to install another king. The true King, in all His glory and sovereign power, will become your life force. Nothing should stand between you and Jesus Christ.

When as a Christian, you place Him on simmer on the back burner of your life, it is like having a royal crown placed on your head, then choosing to leave the royal chambers to work your way to all that the crown offers. A child of the King does not live in the laundry room of the palace.

Today, those who seek the created instead of the Creator have minds as blinded as those who made their own gods thousands of years ago. The Bible records responses of humans that, with simple name changes, locations, and times, would be true in our own lives, communities, churches, and nations today. Many today have allowed themselves to follow false gods straight to hell itself.

The following statement by Ralph Waldo Emerson shows a truth that has been unchanged from early biblical records to the first century to the present day:

The gods we worship write their names on our faces, be sure of that. And a man will worship something—have no doubt about that either. He may think that his tribute is paid in secret in the dark recess of his heart—but it will out. That which dominates will determine his life and character. Therefore, it behooves us to be careful what we worship for what we are worshipping, we are becoming.[1]

In God Almighty's time line, a life on earth is as brief as one of your heartbeats. Today, we are about to close out a second millennium. Surroundings may have changed, but our hearts and responses are no different.

Time is short. We must be prepared now to encounter Jesus. Perhaps He will call His Remnant to Him before the next century even begins. Living as a Remnant is not living as a religious person, although certainly the Remnant people are a worshipful people. Remnant believers know that Jesus Christ is a reality, and He will return.

Remnant life is the set-apart life of those who are in love relationship with God. The relationship results from knowing Him through His Word, prayer, revelations and a heart seeking to obey Him alone.

You must remember that you do not know how many hours you have to remain on this earth. Tomorrow, your days on this earth may end. At any moment, Christ may return, putting a stop to man's rebellion and destruction of the earth. Luke's Gospel, year one A.D., warns us to watch for His return:

> *You also must be ready, because the Son of Man will come at an hour when you do not expect Him.* (Luke 12:40)

Which King Do We Serve Today?

The people of Israel, as you have seen, demanded that God give them a king. We still cry out, "Give us a king!"

"Give us a king," cry out the people of the United States every four years. The pollsters reported the shocking news, before the 1996 election, that righteous codes of behavior were not important to voters. The majority of those polled said trust was not as important as the "king" who would give them the particular financial or personal reward they thought would take care of their needs. The King of Kings surely heard the echoes of the nails pounding into His hands. Those same shouts drove Him to that wooden cross two thousand years before.

A *Time Magazine* article reflected that the year 1996 brought jobs, peace, and a strong economy. However, it was pointed out that the "only things missing in the year were nobility, honor, beauty, moral action, and a sense of how to live in the world."[2] It seems to me that we have missed the real King.

Which king is really being served by many religions today? The Lord God chose Moses, Joshua, and then judges to govern Israel on His behalf.

Moses ran to the desert for forty years, and all the while God had an incredible mission for him. He was living as a simple man who had been set apart by a life in the harsh desert. No doubt Moses thought himself the least likely to come across the burning bush from which God spoke.

Moses led His people out of slavery, according to many reliable sources, about fourteen hundred years before the birth of God Jesus Christ (1446 B.C.). That is approximately 3,500 years before you walked on earth as well.

Joshua led His people across the Jordan River into the Promised Land in the year 1406 B.C. and then led them according to the covenant. Moses and Joshua were Remnant men who taught the generations as God commanded. Moses and Joshua are still names we know as powerful, world-changing men 3,500 years later. They had the heart for keeping a covenant relationship.

God acted through these men because they had Remnant hearts. Today, we must be extremely careful that we, too, serve according to God's moral laws.

The Closed Book

Daily we see the miracles and wonders of God before us. Yet often, the Book given to remind us of the power of God and His daily provisions is ignored. In many homes of those who would call themselves Christians, His Book is not opened all week long.

We, like the Israelites, see the dry desert of our lives and refuse to be refreshed by God's waters. The search for power, happiness, prosperity, and health always ends with unsecured and unsatisfied hearts. Still the Bible is shut tight.

If you could witness all the morning rituals in the homes just up and down your street or in your apartment building, you would probably find very few people taking a moment to thank God for waking up that morning with an opportunity to trust Him with yet another day.

It's amazing how much like the Israelites we can be. The idol of the day may be meeting a work deadline, worrying about traffic, worrying about meals, or worrying about the children. These idols will result in anxiety and rush or depression and fear. Yet His answers are in the closed book, still being ignored.

Accomplishments here and there seem so important, yet a wife or child is not bathed in prayer before the day is started. So much is lost, so little is gained, and so much is missed. Generation after generation lives for the day, never learning that one cannot "seize the day" (or "Carpe Diem") by oneself. The closed Book of Life is ignored.

How can the man who ignores God's command to lead his family really succeed? Is his god the financial resources of the world that he seeks? Will he miss life and end up with illness or death? Will he become dependent on alcohol or drugs to withstand the pressure? Is he only fooling himself? Yes! The will of God is the only perfect and powerful path of life. Our Father created us this way so we could truly be in love relationship with Him. Yet many of us lead doubting and disobedient lives.

What will the Father and Son say to such a man or woman when the inevitable happens? Every person will give an account to God for his or her own life. What about those who rush out each morning without time for God, those who make looks, coffee, TV, or five more minutes of sleep an idol? The hand and eye of God will slowly turn away from the foolish who have wallowed in rebellion. An accounting will also take place for the lives in which God has placed a spouse or child.

Ears can be bent to the enemy of God. He baits with lies about God, just as he did to Adam and Eve. Satan deceived Eve, and she deceived Adam. Adam and Eve chose to allow the Evil One into their lives. They chose to reject the words to them that came out of the mouth of God. They made a decision to bring a curse upon themselves. Each one of us has done the same thing a thousand times since we have been alive. It was not because Eve and Adam were two rotten apples, but because the great free will offer of God exists. Don't blame them. The truth is each one of us would have caused humanity to be cast away from the Garden of Eden. The sin nature was present during the gatherings, through the kings, the exile of the people out of Israel and Judah, the return and restoration of the Remnant, the 400 years of God's angry silence and the coming of Jesus Christ.

The tempter tried to deceive Jesus with his lies:

Then Jesus was led by the Spirit into the desert to be tempted by the devil. After fasting forty days and forty nights, He was hungry. The tempter came to Him and

said, "If you are the Son of God, tell these stones to become
bread." Jesus answered, "It is written: 'Man does not live
on bread alone, but on every word that comes from the
mouth of God.'" (Matthew 4:1–4)

Jesus Christ did not bend His precious ear. He stood firm, as
we should. The Word of God chased the enemy away; the Word
of God defeats him every time.

Only the precious Jesus, God the Son, can be our teacher.
The one and only Son of God was the only One who walked the
earth in the perfect will of God.

Jesus reconciled our sin to the purity of God so we could
overcome the world. Through Him, we are privileged to be
adopted into the family of God. Jesus, not just a good man
(there are many good men); Jesus, not just a prophet (there are
many great prophets); Jesus, not an angel (He created them);
but Jesus, God.

From those moments in the Garden, generations have followed that have bent their ears, hearts, souls and minds to the
deceiver. To this day, the world rejects or ignores those who cry
out for a return to the Lord. Many choose to ignore those who
are announcing the return of our Redeemer.

The chain of life, since creation, has grown in three ways.
The first has been a series of weak links, generation to generation. Secondly, there has been a series of open links that allow
anything to enter and are only loosely held together. Yet, God
has remained in covenant relationship with this world because,
thirdly, a Remnant of the faithful has been linked by a gold
stronger than any earthly metal. The Remnant has been linked
together with integrity and love and has obeyed His will for
thousands of years.

The Remnant may include thousands, millions, or billions on
the day that Jesus Christ gathers them up to Him. Members of

cults, idol worshippers, and self-designed, false Christians will not be among them.

Exiled—Restored—Silence

Unfaithful kings, idolatrous people, and deceitful religious practices in the Promised Land eventually resulted in a great disaster. God continually warned the Israelites to turn their hearts back to Him. When facing trials and struggles, they did turn their hearts to Him. When wars threatened and others conquered them, they turned back to God. However, during prosperity, they bowed to designer gods. Unfortunately they, like we today, turned away time and time again. Those with arrogant hearts thought they actually could make their own way. They proudly credited victory and prosperity to themselves.

The Promised Land, now ruled by the kings, was divided into Israel and Judah. Both would fall. The blessings of God are withheld from the rebellious and unfaithful. Observe the disasters falling upon nation after nation today. Unfaithful to the God of Abraham, Isaac, and Jacob, and rejecting Jesus Christ, they are not under the protective shield of Almighty God:

> *Son of man, if a country sins against Me by being unfaithful and I stretch out My hand against it to cut off its food supply and send famine upon it...how much worse will it be when I send against Jerusalem my four dreadful judgments—sword and famine and wild beasts and plague.*
> (Ezekiel 14:13, 21)

God warns His people that His wrath will fall upon them when the covenant with Him is broken. The people of Israel and Judah suffered under the rule of faithless kings who were covenant breakers. Surely there was a Remnant of faithful Israelites:

Yet there will be some survivors—sons and daughters who will be brought up out of it. They will come to you, and when you see their conduct and their actions, you will be consoled regarding the disaster. (Ezekiel 14:22)

The Lord appointed prophets as His messengers. They were God's special representatives, who confronted the people and told them to remember God and keep His commandments. The prophets also warned them of the consequences of their sins.

The first writings of these prophets are recorded in the book of Isaiah. Isaiah (739–681 B.C.) proclaimed God's Word during the reign of several rulers. He denounced the sins of Israel, Judah and the surrounding nations. Isaiah called for repentance and warned of judgment and punishment. Incredibly, the last chapters speak of restoration. The punishment would be exile and captivity in Assyria and then Babylon. What would happen to the faithful Remnant? Both the spill-out of the Israelites' sin and the purposes of God would send the Remnant into the land of exile as well. God had plans for them, as He does for the faithful who live surrounded by the unfaithful. He did not desert His Remnant:

The Remnant shall return, even the Remnant of Jacob, unto the mighty God. (Isaiah 10:21 KJV)

And it shall come to pass in that day, that the Lord shall set His hand again the second time to recover the Remnant of His people, which shall be left, from Assyria, and from Egypt, and from Pathros, and from Cush, and from Elam, and from Shinar, and from Hamath, and from the islands of the sea. (Isaiah 11:11 KJV)

Will God do any less for His faithful today? No. He will keep His promise to gather His beloved Remnant to Himself. His eye never turns away from His Remnant. Isaiah has left you with powerful, encouraging words:

> *And there shall be an highway for the Remnant of His people, which shall be left, from Assyria; like as it was to Israel in the day that he came up out of the land of Egypt.*
> (Isaiah 11:16 KJV)

God promises to deliver you and me. He has a pathway prepared for us. Through the prophet Isaiah, we find His message of great comfort and hope, the coming Messiah. God promises to send the Messiah and establish His kingdom (Isaiah 53).

Micah, also a pre-exile prophet, began his ministry about 735 B.C. Micah joined Isaiah in revealing the peace in the coming kingdom of God. Interestingly at this time, the divided kingdoms of Israel and Judah were enjoying a time of peace. The rich were imitating the luxurious lifestyles of the pagan nations, while the poor were overtaxed and poverty filled the cities. The nations of the world, claiming a Christian heritage, are the Israel and Judah of today.

Spiritual corruption filled the kingdoms as well. God had commanded that His people care for the poor, the widow, and the alien (strangers, non-Jews). God had given His people, as we recall, specific moral laws in the Sinai Covenant. The Israelites had agreed to obey His laws and serve Him only.

Racing toward punishment and ignoring the Sinai Covenant, the people of Israel and Judah absorbed the vile practice of worshipping the pagan gods. Their practices were not very different from our modern society today. The poor of the world are increasing. Hunger and poverty ravage the nations. Are the rich caring for the widow, the poor and the aliens of the world? How long will God wait before He says, "No more!" to us?

The Remnant today must pay close attention to Micah's prophetic words. The Remnant should be aware that times have not changed, and our worldly kingdoms are racing toward destruction as well. Micah pleaded for the Sinai Covenant to be kept; God's discipline was coming. The prophet's warnings were ignored, with disastrous results to both the nation and the people. You and I certainly need to listen and respond to that warning today.

God's covenant must be obeyed by the Remnant in any country. Those who claim to be Christians must remember God's commands. The non-Remnant leaders and those who merely claim to be Christians still have an opportunity to repent and return. A day of reckoning is coming. God will not put up with the world's ways much longer. The prophets' revelations have been realized throughout the past thousands of years. The truth must reach the world as we race toward the return of the Lord Jesus Christ.

It is time for the covenant relationship to be renewed and a restoration to take place. We do not have to do this through the sacrifice on the altar as in the Old Covenant, because Jesus Christ has stood in the gap. However, just as the Israelites at the Jordan had to choose to take action, so does every person today. The walk across the Jordan was a first step. A living walk in triumph is also a first step.

Micah warned that the nation would not survive due to the overwhelming idolatry and apostasy. Read your newspaper or turn on the national and world news tonight. Nothing has changed.

Injustice, corruption, and defiled worship practices caused the Promised Land's downfall. Micah taught that we must return to the covenant agreed to at Mount Sinai. God requires us to be obedient and to act from a heart of love:

> *He has showed you, O man, what is good. And what does the Lord require of you? To act justly and to love mercy and to walk humbly with your God.* (Micah 6:8)

Though exiled, the people remained in God's care. They had to endure punishment as a means of cleansing and correction. God did not abandon His people. He does not abandon us when He must discipline us as well. He will cleanse and correct us when we have not kept a covenant with Him. God alone is the sovereign ruler and the Creator of man:

> *Look! The Lord is coming from His dwelling place; He comes down and treads the high places of the earth. The mountains melt beneath Him and the valleys split apart, like wax before the fire, like water rushing down a slope. All this is because of Jacob's transgression, because of the sins of the house of Israel.* (Micah 1:3–5)

> *I am planning disaster against this people, from which you cannot save yourselves. You will no longer walk proudly, for it will be a time of calamity.* (Micah 2:3)

Has your life ever been on, what you felt, was a smooth, steady course, and then a storm changed that course? For example, look at the drastic changes in corporations and job security in the United States over the past decades. Workers were once able to trust job security, especially after a number of years with a company. Then auto workers, executives, laborers, and secretaries all began to lose that security. The terms *downsizing, takeover,* and *streamlining* were heard from coast to coast.

Talented and secure people were suddenly without income. Lives were abruptly changed and under terrible stress. These people faced an exile from the lifestyle to which they were accustomed. This is an example of changes we do not expect. We can be tossed about by difficult circumstances, like an exile from a homeland or a sudden loss or illness. These occurrences either get our focus back on Him, or we may decide to stay in Babylon. We can choose to either give up or believe God.

In all circumstances, focus on the Lord God. Crown Him alone as King of your life. Choose covenant life. The reasons for each situation may be varied; I cannot speak for God. He is sovereign, and the world is evil. I do know, however, everything is filtered through the hands of God. I do know that life today mirrors life in Micah's day. Trusting man or idols has not secured us and will not secure us. God's powerful, extended hand is yours to take. Nothing should be between the joining of your hand to God's—no man, religion, or group.

We find two truths in the book of Micah. God will punish disobedience, and salvation and hope is through the Messiah. Disaster was coming, but God would keep His promises to the obedient. A future Messiah meant that God would sustain His own during the most severe trials. There is a promised future:

> *I will surely gather all of you, O Jacob; I will surely bring together the Remnant of Israel. I will bring them together like sheep in a pen, like a flock in its pasture; the place will throng with people.* (Micah 2:12)

God was true to His promise to punish the sins of the nation and the individuals. The people were taken captive and removed from the Promised Land after years of warnings.

However, the Remnant of God heard His unfailing promise to preserve a Remnant for Himself. He has always promised to gather those who are left after cleansing and to be a gentle, protective and providing shepherd to them. The God of Abraham, Isaac and Jacob is always triumphant over sin:

> *"In that day," declares the Lord, "I will gather the lame; I will assemble the exiles and those I have brought to grief. I will make the lame a Remnant, those driven away a strong nation."* (Micah 4:6–7)

Micah was given a powerful vision and words from God. He walked about in mourning, sorrowful about the sickness in the lives of the nation. Immorality of the religious leaders and the exploitation of the people were deeply wounding Micah. The Remnant should be as heart-pierced today. The condition of our society, community, and families should wound our hearts. We must bring the truth of God's love and discipline to the world around us. We may suffer sorrow today, but we must look to the future kingdom of God. That may come tomorrow. The promise revealed by Micah should give the Remnant today hope and confidence:

> *The Remnant of Jacob will be in the midst of many peoples like dew from the Lord, like showers on the grass, which do not wait for man or linger for mankind. The Remnant of Jacob will be among the nations, in the midst of many peoples.* (Micah 5:7–8)

In the year 627 B.C., the prophet Jeremiah also warned of God's coming judgment and captivity of the people. Exile from the Promised Land was looming ahead. Jeremiah was God's messenger to Judah for forty years. He was scorned and persecuted for delivering God's stern messages. Continually, Jeremiah told the people to repent and turn to God, or they would be punished. He then predicted the fall of Jerusalem. This all came to pass.

God calls for His people to be faithful covenant keepers. He deals with rebellion in His time. The descendants of those who crossed the Jordan were exiled into captivity. The Remnant heard God's promise:

> *And I will gather the Remnant of my flock out of all countries whither I have driven them, and will bring them again to their folds; and they shall be fruitful and increase.* (Jeremiah 23:3 KJV)

In the years after the exile (539–520 B.C.), prophets again spoke to the people, reminding them that God requires total obedience to His moral law. At this time, a number of exiles had been allowed to return. They were to build a temple. Many of the people had become accustomed to life in exile. After 70 years, new generations were used to the rule of other nations. They remained in the lands of their captors. A Remnant returned to the land to face famine and hard times and attempt to rebuild, even to rebuild His temple.

A Remnant was restored to Israel. They were no longer to possess the land. The period of restoration required strength, faith and obedience. The Lord was with them. He promised to preserve them:

> *Then Zerubbabel...and Joshua...with all the Remnant of the people, obeyed the voice of the Lord their God, and the words of Haggai the prophet, as the Lord their God had sent him, and the people did fear before the Lord.*
>
> (Haggai 1:12 KJV)

Through the prophet Zechariah, God spoke words to build our hearts and lives upon:

> *For the seed shall be prosperous; the vine shall give her fruit, and the ground shall give her increase, and the heavens shall give their dew; and I will cause the Remnant of this people to possess all these things.*
>
> (Zechariah 8:12 KJV)

These words from God so touched my heart, along with Deuteronomy 32:2 and Micah 5:7, that Discipleship and Evangelism WorldWide (D.E.W.W.) was founded upon them. *"Let My teaching fall like rain and My words descend like dew"* (Deuteronomy 32:2). *"The Remnant of Jacob will be in the midst of many peoples like dew from the Lord"* (Micah 5:7). God so loved His created people and so longed for their hearts to be turned toward Him, that I longed to make Him known through His Word to everyone. Everyone on earth was created to long for Him, but only the Remnant will choose Him. Others will search, be deceived, or worship false prophets, false teachers and/or false gods.

Living as the Remnant is the very best life. He calls for His Word to descend on you like the dew. The prophets confirmed that covenant relationship is the right decision to make. God will meet all your needs, but you must live according to His will. Then He will make this possible.

Will you take an action step today to enter or renew your covenant with the sovereign King? Open your heart more deeply and understand that the Bible has no time limits. God offered restoration to exiles. He offers restoration to you. He seeks all of your heart. Return to Him, and He will honor your heart cry. Choose Him, and you will find life.

What have you chosen in life thus far? Is it to serve the gods of pagans and the lies of the world? You must live in the world system, and there are thoughts, habits, and choices you make to serve yourself. It is time to turn back to God. Confess and ask for His power to change you. Refuse to serve anyone or anything less. Live in triumph!

Old Testament prophets brought the message of God to the people. The last words of the Old Testament foretold the coming of Jesus Christ. The last book of the Old Testament is the book of Malachi, and it, too, proclaims a warning and a hope for us to bind to our hearts and minds:

> *"Surely the day is coming; it will burn like a furnace. All the arrogant and every evildoer will be stubble, and that day that is coming will set them on fire," says the Lord Almighty.* (Malachi 4:1)

(Serious warning to them and to you and me.)

But for you who revere My name, the sun of righteousness will rise with healing in its wings. And you will go out and leap like calves released from the stall....Remember the law of My servant Moses, the decrees and laws I gave him at Horeb for all Israel. (Malachi 4:2, 4)

(Great hope and promise for the Remnant. May this be you and me.)

God then remained silent for 400 years. During that time, the Promised Land was overrun by conquerors. It was a period of great turmoil and change. The Remnant had to cling to the promise that one day God would send the Messiah. Disobedience and apostasy continued among the people. Rulers bowed to other gods, and religious leaders bowed down to self and rulers. The silence of God was, no doubt, deafening.

Notes

1. Simcox, *3000 Quotations on Christian Themes,* p. 32.
2. Rosenblatt, "To Be or Not To Be...Whatever," *Time Magazine* (30 December 1996): p. 105.

Chapter 5

I Promise to Gather You

The Remnant on the earth today comprise the true Church. Christ will one day gather the Remnant into one body, who will be called up by the Savior. *Ekklesia* (Greek for church) actually means "called out." The Church includes all those who are in a saving relationship through and with God Jesus Christ.

Thus the Church, those who have new life in Christ, will be called out of this earth. Christ has promised to return for His beloved men, women, and children. *"Behold, I am coming soon!"* (Revelation 22:7, 12). Only God knows the truly faithful who are His own:

> *In that day the Branch of the Lord will be beautiful and glorious, and the fruit of the land will be the pride and glory of the survivors in Israel. Those who are left in Zion, who remain in Jerusalem, will be called holy, all who are recorded among the living in Jerusalem. The Lord will wash away the filth of the women of Zion; He will cleanse the bloodstains from Jerusalem by a spirit of judgment and a spirit of fire. Then the Lord will create over all of Mount Zion and over those who assemble there a cloud of smoke by day and a glow of flaming fire by night; over all*

the glory will be a canopy. It will be a shelter and shade from the heat of the day, and a refuge and hiding place from the storm and rain. (Isaiah 4:2–6)

According to Romans 8:30, the Remnant has been called to be glorified. This means to be made glorious, to be a man or woman of honor. Through this glorification, you will be giving honor and glory to God the Father. The Savior prayed for this, as His time to be glorified had come (John 12:23). He was willing to take your sin and my sin upon Himself:

Now My heart is troubled, and what shall I say? "Father, save Me from this hour"? No, it was for this very reason I came to this hour. Father, glorify Your name!
(John 12:27–28)

Why Jesus?

Matthew 5:17–18 states that Jesus was not abolishing the Mosaic Law. There were three types of laws given at Sinai: legal, ceremonial, and moral law. Jesus did not come to annul the law of Moses. He fulfilled the law. Jesus said:

Do not think that I have come to abolish the Law or the Prophets; I have not come to abolish them but to fulfill them. I tell you the truth, until heaven and earth disappear, not the smallest letter, not the least stroke of a pen, will by any means disappear from the Law until everything is accomplished. (Matthew 5:17–18)

We, also, are not to do away with the law of Moses. Although we are no longer required to keep the ceremonial laws, by God's grace, we are to keep the legal and moral laws.

A pilot cannot navigate an airplane until he or she is equipped to do so. Those who fly often and, no doubt, those who fly infrequently, expect pilots to know the mechanics of the plane. I count on them to know how and why each complicated instrument in front of them works. Living as a Remnant means becoming personally familiar with the mercy, love, and justice of God. If you as a believer do not personally know the Word of God, and if He is not the first one you trust in every decision, you will crash.

Knowing God does not come simply from a personal experience or hearing someone else's experience. Jesus came so you would personally live in a one-to-one relationship with Him, the Truth. Without exception, no life is excellent without the foundation stone of Jesus Christ.

A life form can be known through its genetic code. We know that a scientist can identify a human being. You are a special creation, created by God to be a human being. You are the one and only of God's specific creations.

Every Remnant person on this earth today has a common identity; Christ Jesus is alive within him or her. The grace and love of Father God, the God of Abraham, Isaac, and Jacob, have provided the key to His kingdom. The great key to triumphant life is the decision to believe that Jesus Christ is God and has been raised alive from the dead. The disciple Peter acknowledged, *"You are the Christ, the Son of the living God"* (Matthew 16:16). Jesus said to Peter and to those who agree, *"I will give you the keys of the kingdom of heaven"* (v. 19).

This is the key to the treasury and the papers that certify your royal position. No degree, work of goodness, or idol can unlock the door to empowered life. The Word of God states, *"If you confess with your mouth, 'Jesus is Lord,' and believe in your heart that God raised Him from the dead, you will be saved"* (Romans 10:9). Paul continued, *"For it is with your heart that you believe"* (v. 10).

Stop! Look! Listen! Remember the words God spoke to the Israelites gathered at the Jordan River: *"Hear now, O Israel!"*

(Deuteronomy 4:1). The command of God rings out in a firm, strong voice: *"Hear!"*

Jesus Christ offers living water to men and women today. The water of the well of that offering was received by a Samaritan woman, who had been taking trips to the wells of the world to find love, peace, direction, and a sense of worth. She found her spiritual thirst satisfied by the living water, Jesus. He found her and loved her heart (John 4).

The Word of God has never changed and has never been disproved. It offers the true food for life. This food and water is necessary for survival, an absolute essential for your life physically and spiritually. Jesus Christ said that He is *"the bread of life"* (John 6:35), and through Him is found life-giving water (John 4:13–14).

The lonely, isolated Samaritan woman encountered the One who knows us and heals us. *"Whoever drinks the water I give him will never thirst"* (John 4:14). Jesus Christ promised to restore and refresh us with His life-giving water, as He did for that woman who was mired in sin. So are the rest of us without Him. Feeling alive and new, she testified what He had done for her, and many others were drawn to Jesus. Many times, we hear the testimony of this woman in teachings that stop short of a very important point. John 4:39–42 confirms that many believed because of what Jesus Christ had done in her life, but believers are called to take the next step. Go directly to Jesus personally.

The woman's testimony opened other hearts, and the new believers went to Jesus Christ Himself to learn the truth. Many more believed because of His own Word: *"And said unto the woman, Now we believe, not because of thy saying: for we have heard Him ourselves, and know that this is indeed the Christ, the Saviour of the world"* (John 4:42 KJV).

Have you thought of yourself as religious? Have you given your life to a God you have not known in hopes of getting through the gates of heaven when you die? Has your life changed since you decided to be a Christian? Have you heard Him?

Perhaps you have assumed, as many dangerously have, that because your parents took you to church as an infant to a religious event such as a christening, you are a Christian. However, a decision for Jesus Christ means just that—you personally give up your life to God through God the Son, Jesus Christ.

I recall meeting many men and women in a former northern Soviet State and in Eastern Europe who time and again said they were Christians because they had been christened in a church as a baby. These were beautiful and sincere people. Many indeed, after fifty years of forbidden teaching, were just now realizing the need to personally seek the Lord Jesus Christ.

Many shared that their grandmothers had taken them to the ceremony and also told them about church. It was a great blessing to see the fruit produced through the faithfulness of many oppressed women. They were the spiritual life of the family behind the closed door of communism. Then the 1989 Revolution changed the world and allowed the Gospel and Bible to be shared in the former Soviet Union. Hearts were thirsty to learn more about life and love in Jesus Christ through His Word.

I was mightily blessed to be welcomed to speak and to teach the seekers of truth. They could now make an informed and prepared decision to give their lives to Jesus. God's Word was no longer illegal in many countries. The thirsty were able to freely and openly drink of His living water, Jesus.

Never had I imagined that God had been preparing me through the hurting years, the rebellious years, the marvelous years, and the learning years, preparing me for such a time as this. The magnitude of God's forgiveness and love is evidenced by how He has blessed me.

God did not demand a relationship, but He called out, "Hear, O Israel!" God calls the same to you. Hear and know the offer and the commands of obedience, the blessings and the curses. The greatest news of all is that He loved you enough to take your sins upon Himself when God the Son Jesus Christ made the decision to be your sacrificial offering (John 3:16).

The apostle Paul brought the good news to the synagogue rulers in Antioch: Jesus Christ God came to earth and was persecuted, killed on the cross, and buried in a garden tomb. God raised Him from the dead, and He was seen from Galilee to Jerusalem by those who had been with Him. Jesus was raised from the dead, never to decay (Acts 13:34). He lives and will gather the Remnant.

You are called to hear and to responsibly know God. Why is this of great importance to you? So that, at this moment, you might choose to take this opportunity to examine your heart and make a decision for life. All you need to do is ask for forgiveness for your life apart from Him. Ask Jesus to come into your heart as your personal Savior.

This is a choice for life, not one of works. Because you went to Sunday school as a child or because your family joined a church does not make you a Christian. A decision has not been made if you feel that going to a church every Sunday will result in eternal life.

Your decision to become reconciled to God through Jesus Christ does mean you are saved from the eternal lake of fire. Eternal blessings begin with fullness during your earthly journey. Know for sure that church does not save and family does not save. Your decision to give your heart to God, allowing Him to restore you, heal you, love you, and lead you, will save you. This, without question, is the moment in time that is the most important of your earthly life.

If you are afraid that you have done so much wrong or that you can't measure up, then know that God's mercy covers that. The Holy Spirit will change your heart and speak truth to you if you ask Him. Jesus looks for you to repent of your sin. First John 1:9 assures you of forgiveness and cleansing:

> *If we confess our sins, He is faithful and just and will forgive us our sins and purify us from all unrighteousness.*

Do you believe that you really are both forgiven and cleansed when your heart is given to Jesus?

One night, following a meeting where people had been invited to come forward and ask Jesus into their hearts, a woman struck up a conversation with me. I share this story so you won't walk in uncertainty.

She exclaimed that she loved to be at these meetings and "went up every night to ask Jesus into her heart." Had she not heard that once you believe and ask Jesus Christ into your heart He saves you? Yes, she had, but she could not accept that He actually did this for her, so she needed to make sure every time.

In some churches, I recognize several people who go forward at every service and at every call to the altar. They must be very confused about their position in Christ. What troubles these people, and what does their church teach them? These people are not walking in the Father's blessed assurance and are not believing that God forgives the repentant heart (1 John 1:9). Victory and healing are ours in Christ.

We have one life to give and then it is His, but this woman insisted that it was a "good feeling" to get saved every night. Are you in such a place? Is it possible your heart needs to believe His promise?

Remember, Romans 10:9–10 reveals, *"If you confess with your mouth, 'Jesus is Lord,' and believe in your heart that God raised Him from the dead, you will be saved."* Salvation is a gift from God; you do not have to work for it. Ask, and He takes your heart to His.

Think of the Shepherd Jesus Christ's caring and compassionate heart for people, for you. Think of the sorrow of the heart of Jesus when He stood on a hill above Jerusalem and wept for those who rejected God (Luke 19:41–44). What they missed! They were no longer gathered in His presence and guidance, and many were about to gather to crucify God. Please make sure today you will not be counted among the foolish or lost.

Wonderful news! Jesus Christ died to reconcile you to our Holy Father. There is no other Father for you but the Great and Almighty God. *"I am Alpha and Omega, the beginning and the ending, saith the Lord, which is, and which was, and which is to come, the Almighty"* (Revelation 1:8 KJV). Triumphant life is made possible by the Father's love and Jesus Christ's powerful victory through the cross. *"And having disarmed the powers and authorities, He made a public spectacle of them, triumphing over them by the cross"* (Colossians 2:15).

How does the Remnant live in triumph? God's plans for you have been clearly stated in His Word. History changes, scientific theories change, philosophies change, and fads or cults change; but the Alpha and Omega (Revelation 1:8) never changes. His plans and guidance have always been clear. The prophets and the written Word of God have never been disproved and have never changed. We need not wonder about living a triumphant life, beloved reader. It is already a reality, if you choose it.

You can choose His code of ethics and live in His power. Colossians chapters 3 and 4 make it easy to understand the great way and the only way. After choosing Christ as your Savior, you will have a heart change, a desire to live for Him alone. *"God made* [you] *alive together with Him, having forgiven* [you] *all* [y]*our trespasses"* (Colossians 2:13 RSV).

"Set your minds on things that are above" (Colossians 3:2 RSV), the Lord commands, because the believer has been raised with Christ who is seated at the right hand of God. Then there

is action, empowered by the Holy Spirit, after your heart has cried out to love God.

The Day of the Lord
Sunrise...Sonrise

Men of Israel, and you that fear God, listen. The God of this people Israel chose our fathers and made the people great during their stay in the land of Egypt, and with up-lifted arm He led them out of it. And for about forty years He bore with them in the wilderness. And when He had destroyed seven nations in the land of Canaan, He gave them their land as an inheritance, for about four hundred and fifty years. And after that He gave them judges until Samuel the prophet. Then they asked for a king; and God gave them Saul the son of Kish, a man of the tribe of Benjamin, for forty years. And when He had removed him, He raised up David to be their king; of whom He testified and said, "I have found in David the son of Jesse a man after My heart, who will do all My will." Of this man's posterity God has brought to Israel a Savior, Jesus, as He promised. Before His coming John had preached a baptism of repentance to all the people of Israel. And as John was finishing his course, he said, "What do you suppose that I am? I am not He. No, but after me One is coming, the sandals of whose feet I am not worthy to untie." Brethren, sons of the family of Abraham, and those among you that fear God, to us has been sent the message of this salvation. For those who live in Jerusalem and their rulers, because they did not recognize Him nor understand the utterances of the prophets which are read every Sabbath, fulfilled these by condemning Him. Though they could charge Him with nothing deserving death, yet they asked Pilate to have Him killed. And when they had fulfilled all that was written of Him, they took Him down from the tree, and laid Him in a tomb. But God raised Him from the dead; and for many days He appeared to those who came up with Him from Galilee to Jerusalem, who are now His witnesses to the people. And we bring you the good news that what God promised to the fathers, this He has fulfilled to us their children by raising Jesus; as also it is written in the second psalm, "Thou art My Son, today I have begotten Thee." And as for the fact that He raised Him from the dead, no more to return to corruption, He spoke in this way, "I will give you the holy and sure blessings of David." Therefore He says also in another psalm, "Thou wilt not let Thy Holy One see corruption." For David, after he had served the counsel of God in his own generation, fell asleep, and was laid with his fathers, and saw corruption; but He whom God raised up saw no corruption. Let it be known to you therefore, brethren, that through this Man forgiveness of sins is proclaimed to you, and by Him every one that believes is freed from everything from which you could not be freed by the law of Moses. Beware, therefore, lest there come upon you what is said in the prophets: "Behold, you scoffers, and wonder, and perish; for I do a deed in your days, a deed you will never believe, if one declares it to you." (Acts 13:16–41 RSV)

The great news is that God continues to make Himself known. He became flesh and dwelt among us (John 1:14) to preserve the Remnant for Himself. God the Son dwelt among us, paid for all the sins of those who surrender their lives to Him, and made an intimate relationship with God the Father a reality for the Remnant:

For God so loved the world [you] that He gave His only begotten Son, that whosoever believeth in Him should not perish, but have everlasting life. (John 3:16 KJV)

God, the Covenant Keeper, has opened the door for your relationship with Him today in keeping with the majestic promise:

*I have loved you with an everlasting love; I have drawn
you with loving-kindness.*   (Jeremiah 31:3)

This promise was made about 600 years before He, God Jesus, came to earth to reconcile you to your Father. The Covenant Keeper is always preserving and gathering His Remnant.

The Word of God Jesus, when believed in your heart, is a sunrise to your heart just as the sunrise over the Red Sea was seen by
Moses and the Israelites. I have a photograph of the sun rising
over the Red Sea, and to me it is full of meaning. The sun in the
picture, as it brings light to the earth, is a confirmation of God's
power and faithfulness. The path of light that shines on the water
reflects the direct walk to the mighty Light, Jesus Christ. Christ
rose again to bring daylight to you instead of darkness.

All this has been made possible for you and me through the
dark death and radiant Sonrise 2,000 years ago. God's faithfulness is awesome to those who choose to ask Him into their
hearts. You and I no longer have to try to become holy on our
own. Beloved, you are set apart by God through faith by believing Him. The bodily-resurrected Jesus Christ assured a doubting apostle called Thomas, *"Put your finger here; see my hands.
Reach out your hand and put it into my side. **Stop doubting
and believe***" (John 20:27, emphasis added).

Indeed, stop doubting and believe. Allow the Sonlight of God
to rise upon you the rest of your life.

How understanding of Father God. He knew those He loved
would doubt that a crucified man could be wholly and fully
raised three days after His heart stopped. There were many
years when I thought this was absolute nonsense. I thought the
Red Sea crossing and the resurrection were just stories, so rebellious was my own heart. Until the Lord spoke to my mind
and heart, I missed the fact that the tomb was empty. There
never has been any proof that Jesus' body was stolen or buried.

> This fraudulent transaction [in Matthew 28:11–15] proceeds upon the admission by the enemies of Christianity that the grave was empty—an admission which is enough to show that the evidence for the empty grave was "too notorious to be denied."[1]

Sparrow-Simpson argues that "The emptiness of the grave is acknowledged by opponents as well as affirmed by disciples."[2]

The apostle Thomas was a man who needed proof. No doubt, I was standing right alongside of him, as I am one who is as wary as can be of the claims of man. They must be validated by His Word. My first action as an educator or writer has always been to evaluate the source, motives, background, and evidence of the claimant. Thomas asked the resurrected Jesus to prove He really was the man who had been killed and buried.

Thomas, who was actually called Didymus, meaning "twin," has many spiritual twins today. Thomas missed the meeting of the faithful when Jesus first appeared to them, so he would not believe them. He wanted to see for himself. Some may see this as obstinate. In light of the swarms of lying dark spirits who sound plausible today, God demonstrates to you and me that He will personally make Himself known to us with His presence. Even if you have missed opportunity after opportunity to know Him, He will still be there when you seek Him.

You can have a "Thomas experience" at the moment your heart desires to personally know Jesus Christ as your risen Savior. Christ is our personal Savior. Ask for yourself as Thomas did. God has many ways of making Himself known, and He knows those who are truly seeking Him.

Thomas was honest with Jesus. Jesus gave Thomas sure knowledge of Himself and the reality of the resurrection. He had missed the gathering of disciples on the day that Jesus *"came and stood among them"* (John 20:19).

The same missed opportunities can happen when a follower decides to miss worship with other believers. This is not to say there cannot be a reason to miss a time of worship, but even then we could miss an enormous blessing. Actually, after the death of Jesus, His disciples, according to John 20:19, had fearfully gathered behind closed doors. They were fearful without Him. How we need the comfort and closeness of those who love Jesus when circumstances seem very dangerous. The Remnant of God, the faithful, need to do the same today. What happened then is what happens now: Jesus shows up and gives us the blessing of peace, calms our fears, and becomes our strength (John 20:20).

John described the group of Jesus' disciples, known followers of Christ who walked with Him and lived in His presence. It was certainly understandable that they were fearful after the cross, considering what had happened at Calvary. They did not imagine Jesus would appear to them bodily.

You and I have the blessing of being able to read John's Gospel. We read that Jesus came into a locked room through the wall and stood among them (John 20:19). We read the testimony of what happened. Do not make the mistake of seeking answers, comfort, and peace from those who are not disciples or from those who may be deceiving you in doctrine or lifestyle.

Thomas could actually put his hand into Christ's spear-pierced side. One fact that convinced me of the truth of the Bible was that I realized that Thomas never recanted his story, nor did any others. Would you withstand years of persecution and accusation because of a lie? Not me, that is for sure. Thomas never gave in to the many offers to recant his experience. How the Romans and unbelieving Jews would have offered Thomas "the world" for a retraction. I'm sure he suffered a great deal to speak the truth. There can be no wiser decision but to say to Jesus, as Thomas did, *"My Lord and my God!"* (John 20:28).

The Remnant believer looks to the face of Christ and always calls out the same: *"My Lord and my God!"*

The day the Lord Jesus Christ returns to earth will be spectacular. The Word of God tells us of the final gathering of His faithful Remnant:

> *At that time men will see the Son of Man coming in clouds with great power and glory. And He will send His angels and gather His elect from the four winds, from the ends of the earth to the ends of the heavens.* (Mark 13:26–27)

Biblical prophecy has been proved accurate. World events continue to unfold toward the day Christ puts an end to the present world systems. For the men, women and children who have been saved through Christ, it will be the greatest joy they have ever known. For those who have scoffed, blasphemed and rejected Him, it will be a day worse than Armageddon.

Jesus Christ died to forgive your sins and to reconcile you to God. God cannot violate His own law (Himself), so He cannot have a relationship with sin. Sin does not come from Satan's deceit or schemes alone, but from our own sinful nature. Man has always broken God's law, but the Remnant's heart longs to be obedient in spite of his or her own nature.

The covenant agreement given through Moses at Mount Sinai detailed God's moral laws. Man was to keep these, but he did not, so God turned away from man (Hebrews 8:7–9). Jesus, the Reconciler, brought the New Covenant, and He is the High Priest and mediator of it:

> *I will put My laws in their minds and write them on their hearts. I will be their God, and they will be My people.*
> (Hebrews 8:10)

Notes

1. James Hastings, *The Dictionary of the Apostolic Church,* vol. 2 (Edinburgh: T&T Clark, 1918), p. 507.

2. Hastings, Selbie, and Lambert, eds., *A Dictionary of Christ and the Gospels,* vol. 2 (New York: Scribner's Sons, 1909), p. 508.

Chapter 6

God Is Faithful

The Lord is faithful to all His promises and loving toward all
He has made....The Lord is righteous in all His ways and loving
toward all He has made. The Lord is near to all who call on
Him....The Lord watches over all who love Him.
—Psalm 145:13, 17, 18, 20

G od is an infinite and eternal being. He is purely spiritual,
with supreme personal intelligence, the Creator of all
things. He is the perfect moral ruler; God alone is to be worshipped. God is tri-personal, the Father, Son, and Holy Spirit.[1]

You can trust God. He alone is absolutely faithful. His faithfulness to righteous people is confirmed in His Word:

Know therefore that the Lord your God is God; He is the
faithful God, keeping His covenant of love to a thousand
generations of those who love Him and keep His com-
mands. But those who hate Him He will repay to their

face by destruction; He will not be slow to repay to their
face those who hate Him.   (Deuteronomy 7:9–10)

This is both a promise and warning to be heeded seriously.

The splendor of an early morning sunrise radiates across the Nevada desert as rose-colored light slowly turns the landscape into golden brilliance. Rising above the eastern mountain ranges, the sun is a reminder to all that a new day has come. The rising sun is a sign of the faithfulness of an ever present God. He set the earth in rotation at just the degree needed for all the earth to have the light that He created. God, the great *"I AM"* (Exodus 3:14), who causes the sun to rise each morning and to set every evening, calls you to turn your heart totally toward Him alone. The Israelites, like many today, chose to have a designer god who would fit their needs. Their god spread darkness over their daily lives. Day by day, they shrouded their minds and lived in increasing darkness. Nothing has changed. We live in the rebellious land as well.

If you attend a church, does your faith depend upon the visibility of a particular leader, minister, pastor, or priest? God's message states that each person must have a personal encounter with God the Father, Son, and Holy Spirit through His Word. Those who depend upon man or upon an experiential faith are chasing the wind. If you have never come to know Him through His revelation of Himself in the Word, I encourage you to write for the D.E.W.W. Bible Study information, or please write to me personally to inquire more about Him.

Being all wise, God, in His love for those He created, gave specific directions to His Remnant people through Moses at Sinai in the Ten Commandments and the laws of life. Moses then prepared the people forty years later by calling the Remnant to obedience of those laws and moral codes. God made promises that He will keep to the obedient.

God Is Faithful

God's Commands to Israel

You shall have no other gods before me.	Exodus 20:3
You shall not make any graven image.	Exodus 20:4
You shall not take the name of the Lord your God in vain.	Exodus 20:7
Remember the Sabbath day by keeping it holy.	Exodus 20:8
Honor your father and mother.	Exodus 20:12
You shall not kill.	Exodus 20:13
You shall not commit adultery.	Exodus 20:14
You shall not steal.	Exodus 20:15
You shall not bear false witness.	Exodus 20:16
You shall not covet.	Exodus 20:17

The Lord will establish you as His holy people, as He promised you on oath, if you keep the commands of the Lord your God and walk in His ways. (Deuteronomy 28:9)

Why did God require His people to obey His laws, and why does He demand the same from you now?

Then all the peoples on earth will see that you are called by the name of the Lord, and they will fear you.
(Deuteronomy 28:10)

His absolute plan for you is that when people see you as an individual, they will know you are a set-apart Remnant man or woman of God. So there are two choices: First, you choose to give Him your life, and second, you choose to know God. Those who make these choices receive the blessings of God:

> *All these blessings will come upon you and accompany you if you obey the Lord your God: You will be blessed in the city and blessed in the country. The fruit of your womb will be blessed, and the crops of your land and the young of your livestock....Your basket and your kneading trough will be blessed. You will be blessed when you come in and blessed when you go out.* (Deuteronomy 28:2–6)

A promise is made to you and me by God. A strong command accompanies this promise:

> *If you pay attention to the commands of the Lord your God that I give you this day and carefully follow them, you will always be at the top, never at the bottom. Do not turn aside from any of the commands I give you today, to the right or to the left, following other gods and serving them.* (Deuteronomy 28:13–14)

If you follow the ways of God, the first and foremost superhighway of life is open to you. The road map is clearly laid out through the Word of God. *"There will be a highway for the Remnant of His people"* (Isaiah 11:16). I believe you can choose whether you are going to travel in a Rolls Royce or on a stationary bicycle. You may even be walking slowly, but with a heart that both needs and wants the Triune God. You may be in a spiritual passage where you long for a deeper relationship or a deep healing of a doubtful or broken heart. You can choose to travel on the superhighway.

Perhaps this is the moment to seek Him with all your heart so you will be found by Him, as promised in Jeremiah 29:13. You may be seeking a more powerful mode of travel for your life, ready to experience more "horsepower" as you travel. God is the Knower of your Heart:

> *Then hear Thou from heaven Thy dwelling place, and forgive, and render unto every man according unto all his ways, whose heart Thou knowest; (for Thou only knowest the hearts of the children of men.)* (2 Chronicles 6:30 KJV)

Only God, your intimate and loving Father, knows what is troubling, what is painful and what you cry out for today. He will provide the power for you to be healed. I rely on the fact that God knows my heart. He will care for me and meet me wherever I am. He is raising me up to live in triumph.

God gave us hearts of warriors. Joshua and David showed us the fortitude and strength God gives us. This is available to you through Christ and the Holy Spirit. Claim your Joshua and David heart within you, because God does not fill you with fear and weakness. When given the controls, God will empower you with all He offers.

It is God's will that an obedient follower be blessed. Deuteronomy 28:12 states, *"The Lord will open the heavens, the storehouse of His bounty, to send rain on your land in season and to bless all the work of your hands."*

Are you expecting God to keep His promises? I think some believers have stopped along life's highway because they have the wrong expectations. A stop sign has been planted by a lack of believing in God's promises. A giant stop sign, with a pole named "lack of faith," blocks a triumphant life.

No matter what the earthly trials, the Remnant can stand on the promises of the opened heavens and the bounty of God's storehouse to flow into their lives. God promises He will do this for the obedient believer. God intends for His relationship with you to be intimate and personal. His promise is to establish you as His holy people (Deuteronomy 28:9). No matter what the circumstances, cling to and believe in the Word of God.

Doug was a strong, vital, athletic man who coached baseball on the college level. He was also my husband. In his late forties, he was diagnosed with Lou Gehrig's disease (A.L.S.) and died approximately 14 months later. A.L.S. ravages the neurological system and requires constant care. The Lord was a powerful presence during this time. When one's life is interrupted unexpectedly, it can devastate the emotions if God is absent.

Difficult as it was, I rarely had a moment to think about my future. Vague thoughts of what life as a widow would mean were interrupted by the moment-by-moment care and crises.

Doug entrusted his illness to the Lord during his brave struggle. I believe it is a merciful act of God when we don't know what times such as this will be like. We both tried to live each day as God gave it to us. We knew that God was in control. He would absolutely heal Doug, either in this faulty, diseased world or in His eternal kingdom. I fully believe that God's will is for His people to be well. I also believe God is sovereign, and every life belongs to Him. He knows the day that each of us will be with Him.

I watched Doug's faith grow stronger and deeper as the disease progressed. I experienced a God whom I could talk to about each worry, pain, and exhausting day. Even though I myself had tremendous recurring pain from a severe neck injury, He was my strength as promised.

We had recently moved to the high desert in the eastern Sierra Nevada Mountains. I believe with my whole heart that God led us there. He was about to give Doug the great joy of meeting

Him face-to-face. Doug, I knew, would soon run again as in the days of his youth.

When he died, I held him, and the Lord whispered in my ear that this separation was "just for a moment." He also said, "I have a work for you to do, Priscilla." He gave me the picture of Doug running toward Him with a strong new body, of Doug hitting long home runs to the outfield of heaven.

Several days later, I realized that I was able to do most anything I chose now. My tired self tried to sort out my future plans. During Doug's illness there were few to help, but God had always provided. How could I ever really describe the days of progressive paralysis, choking and total care? It was only through the mercy and compassion of God that I was able to bear it. He was preparing me to tackle whatever came along with Him.

The important thing was the faithfulness of God. He knew what He wanted for us during that time. We sought God in a deeper way. I found myself less and less able to do anything without prayer.

I share all this not because of the suffering and the long desert period in my life which followed, but because I experienced God's strength and His love. During my life as an atheist, people had rarely let me down. I knew how to recognize those who lived for themselves or those whose ethics reeked like a town dump.

The people I knew outside of my family usually could be trusted; they usually had compassion and understanding and respect. I could count on many who would be ignored in Christian circles today. I know that God knew me every day of those years and would use all my fleshly and worldly experiences for His good. Romans 8:28 promises that He will use everything *"for the good of those who love Him."* Now, as a woman who believed and loved God, I was alone. God had sent me to a barren desert.

A desert experience for the Remnant man or woman can be the greatest opportunity to come to a heart knowledge of God. Often we find bankruptcy, terminal illness, prison, or the loss of a spouse or child to be a time in a desert. However, a desert experience can be the time during which you will most clearly understand God's deep, steadfast love and compassion.

All of life has two sides, beautiful mountaintops and dark valleys of tears. My life has been filled with varied and rich experiences. God has blessed me with love from His Remnant in mighty ways.

When I was in that desert, I did not realize, at first, that God was building my strength and discernment. He taught me to recognize those who truly sought Him and His Word. He prepared me to take Him out to the world.

The struggles were immense. I thought for many years, as a high school teacher and then as a college professor, my contribution to life would be building strong lives through the word of man. I felt I had realistic expectations. After surviving a violent childhood of mixed messages of religion and abandonment, I felt I could help a hurting world.

I rejected God and sought solutions to the end of cruelty, wars, poverty, and persecution in the world. Surely, the wisdom of scholars past and present provided insight into these problems. I did not realize that there were actually two very different systems.

The world *(Gr. kosmos)* can be defined as the present condition of human affairs in alienation and opposition to God.[2] *"We have not received the spirit of the world but the Spirit who is from God"* (1 Corinthians 2:12).

Concerning the world's *(Gr. aiōn)* characteristics, a believer is commanded, *"Do not conform any longer to the pattern of this world, but be transformed by the renewing of your mind"* (Romans 12:2).

God must have been distressed by my futile pursuits in my own strength, yet He waited for the moment I would choose to listen quietly to Him and allow Him to rescue me. Looking back, I see He protected me from a life in the wrong lane. He allowed me to walk along many a cliff's edge but caught me each time I was ready to fall. All the while, I scoffed and mocked at the idea of a real Jesus on a real cross. I had seen the religious in action in my family and society and wanted no part of it.

Later, while married and raising two daughters, thinking I was exactly where I wanted and needed to be, I encountered Jesus Christ. Here was the answer to the problems and behaviors of man. God had a plan for mankind from the beginning, a perfect relationship with Him. He was the Source of Life, the Provider, the Lover, the Protector. He was not a destroyer of those who were in relationship with Him. He was more wounded by the actions of man in history than I had ever been.

My Father created me and had His purpose for me. Although I missed out for many years, I could be born again into relationship life in Christ. I felt I had surfaced from life underwater and had found pure air at last. I felt a peace beyond what I could have imagined. I learned Jesus Christ was returning for His people, His covenant keepers. The world's violence, illness, greed, and death would cease. Peace, harmony, and new life were available. I would not find them in a human relationship, but only in Him. When you are born again by asking Jesus Christ to become your Savior, your mind becomes renewed.

To the faithful Remnant, an obedient people, God will be faithful. Your career, marriage, relationships, and finances are all empowered by God on the Remnant road. A man or woman who halfheartedly serves the Lord or occasionally honors Him, while striving toward personal success in career and finance, will never achieve what would have been achieved with God Almighty.

You are responsible to spend time with God and the Word of God. This is the key to an intimate relationship. The Word keeps you from turning to the right or left or from following the false teacher. Man's manipulative teachings have stolen minds from the beginning. Satan's manipulation of Adam and Eve is recorded so that you will take to heart what the Evil One does with the human mind. A relationship with God must acknowledge Christ as God, the Savior. The Word of God is your shield and your belt of truth.

There are doubters of God who say that this life is filled with such trouble that the blessings of the opened heavens cannot be true. There are those who claim God will make us prosperous, and tell us that to gain financial prosperity, we just give money. Only God will judge those who teach anything that falls away from the plumb line. You are commanded to give your tithes to Him (Malachi 3:8–12). All belongs to Him. He blesses obedience to His commands.

God is sovereign. *"The Most High is sovereign over the kingdoms of men"* (Daniel 4:25). He has promised to be faithful to those who are faithful. Those people, the Remnant, will receive His blessings. Will God bless the unrighteous more than His beloved son or daughter? No.

God does not promise His children blessings and then deny them. A human father may have done this in your life. You may have been let down by a pastor, a Christian, or a close family member, but God loves perfectly and justly.

God offers you the rights to become His child. Beloved reader, you have the rights to the kingdom's promises today! God does not and will not fail you. Your own natural spirit will fail you if you rely upon it, but the Holy Spirit will not be unfaithful to His beloved.

A friend shared this personal account of God's answer to her prayers:

After many years of praying for my four children to be saved and to be committed Christians, I received a word from the Lord that instructed me to place my children at the foot of the Cross, to take my hands off, to stop trying to do the impossible in my own strength. God said to me, "Give Me the reins and I will rein them in as I will."

This was not easy for me to do, because I am a fixer of everyone's problems. Until now I made a big mess of things, thinking I was helping. I was at the end of my rope, until I made a decision to trust Him all the way.

God is moving in a mighty way, and one by one, they are coming to Him. Praise God! He is faithful to His Word. What freedom I feel, knowing He is in control and I don't have to fret anymore. The work, I know now, is as good as done when we let Him take the reins. My fixing did not repair relationships. My fixing was blocking God's answers.[3]

Is joy one of God's blessings? How many do you know who have a deep, contented joy? How many parents do you know who model God's caring love to their children? I know many parents who do not have a peaceful heart about the safety and security of their children. There is a canyon of difference between temporary pleasure and the everlasting joy in covenant relationship. *"Do not lean on your own understanding"* (Proverbs 3:5 NAS). Find the joy, love, and peace in parenting.

Many men and women in corporate America or in general business have little job security. Unbelievers fear cutbacks in employment. God will be there with His plan to provide and protect them. The Remnant believer can absolutely rely on that. All men and women need God's security. All men and women need a trustworthy God, the God of Abraham, Isaac, and Jacob, God Jesus Christ.

At times, I have had to be on the very edge of a crumbling cliff to learn that I truly can rely on His promises. Often this has been the best place for me to learn that it was God's provision and faithfulness that saved me. My own wisdom or actions never saved me from a fall. When we give up self-sufficiency, we can experience a glorious freedom and a new awareness of God's provision.

Discovering the reality of God's personal word to you will change your life. God has shown us the results of turning our hearts toward Egypt, like the Israelites did after the miracle of deliverance from Egyptian slavery. The Word of God reveals His mercy and His absolute justice. God keeps His covenants to those who are faithful. God's faithfulness is proved throughout the Scriptures.

The apostle Paul explained, generations later, the vital importance of the Word of God in your life:

> *For everything that was written in the past was written to teach us, so that through endurance and the encouragement of the Scriptures we might have hope.* (Romans 15:4)

In His Word you will find the personal strength to endure the struggles of your pilgrimage through life. To be sure, you will face hardships, disappointments, and crises in this lifetime. Only in the personal knowledge of the faithfulness of God can you endure with hope.

The Bible is not about selective history lessons. The people on the bank of the Jordan were choosing to cross to a new life. A covenant had been made between God and man. A parallel to their actions and reactions could probably be written in a personal history of my life and yours. Certainly, I have had to learn many hard lessons about full obedience to God. God outlined the blessing for obedience, but He left no room for doubt about the curses for determining your own ways or choosing to ignore God:

You will be cursed in the city and cursed in the country.
Your basket and your kneading trough will be cursed. The
fruit of your womb will be cursed, and the crops of your
land, and the calves of your herds and the lambs of your
flocks. You will be cursed when you come in and cursed
when you go out.   (Deuteronomy 28:16–19)

During this present age, as we are awaiting the return of Christ, the forces of darkness intensify Satan's battle against God. Like tornadoes, they swirl about the earth trying to catch up as many hearts as possible into chaos. Those who live in the Great Plains of the United States know to look out for the dark, vicious funnel clouds. These clouds that touch down in twisted fury capture everything that is not protected.

My deepest prayer for you, beloved reader, is that you will learn about Him from Him. I believe with all my heart that God's way is the only way to experience life's most powerful journey. There is no other reason for my ministry. He has given me life, and He will give you life. Ask for His powerful reality in your life.

Will you be swept up in the dark winds of any storm, or are you a sure Remnant believer of God, solidly protected by the radiance of His Glory?

Built, Broken, and Breached

Have you ever faced a seemingly impossible situation? Has a wall loomed before you and stopped you in your tracks? It has happened to me many times. Sometimes I have chosen to take the wrong turn, away from the highway of holiness, and have found myself struggling on a treadmill before a dead-end wall.

Walls are built by any idols, thoughts, or actions outside the will of God. They may seem acceptable, as we build them into our lives, but these walls block our journey with God. A wall is a barrier.

Worse yet, there can be times when we unexpectedly slam into a stone wall. Usually, this is the result of depending on self or deliberately ignoring God's will. We try to get through the wall, around the wall or over the wall, and we end up with more than a few bloody scrapes and blisters.

Occasionally, there is a wall that seems a bit more giving, so we stand before it, vaguely aware that we need God. We are similar to the Israelites, who may have been daydreaming when the great voice of God rang out, *"Hear, O Israel"* (Deuteronomy 6:4). Bank accounts, job security, homes, fitness programs, retirement plans, and hard work year after year—for many, these are absolutes that build protective life walls. These walls will keep out the enemy and allow us to feel secure in a world of broken boundaries, or so we think.

In a valley along the Moselle River, surrounded by hills of fruitful vineyards, the city of Trier, Germany, has a rich history. Founded as a Roman settlement in 16 B.C., Trier became the capitol of the western Roman Empire by the third century A.D. The city also became a center of early Christianity. The Romans brought their sophistication and superb skills to the area. A city gate from the second century and an incredible system of Roman baths and gardens from the fourth century stand proudly as a testament to the past.

Trier is close to several American military installations where I have been privileged to speak. Ministering outside the country always brings to my mind the fact that the world is small indeed. Traditions may differ, but we are one group of created beings. Our behaviors, hopes and struggles do not differ. The Remnant lives today throughout the world. The Remnant has lived through the lifelines of history, willingly keeping their covenant with God.

Talents, time, and works of man fade, just as God said they would. Only the ruins remain to witness the power gained and the power faded. Walking along the ruins, I became aware that the way of the Lord and His Remnant stands as strong today as it did at the Jordan. Years of change have not breached the walls of God. Mankind's response to God has assaulted His walls, but His strength will never be broken.

The powerful Roman Empire was strong in human terms, depending on their own strength for security. For many years, the Barbarians, as the Germanic tribes were known, sat across the Rhine River in Germany, unable to cross and attack the Roman walls. In the fifth century A.D., a bitter winter changed history. The Germanic tribes raced across a frozen Rhine River to storm the Roman camps and established towns. Trier was conquered, and the Roman Empire was overtaken.

These battles remind me of the battles fought within us, battles that want to put an end to or a detour in our walk on the Lord God's highway. When we experience unexpected, fierce attacks or changes in circumstances, our defenses are weakened. Attacks can defeat us when we build our life walls with false materials.

As an atheist college professor, I certainly tried to get a grasp on the behavior of man only through a secular view. I must say I spent most of those years quite discouraged, because I realized we both build and destroy societies. Societies rise and fall in the same way a pendulum swings. At one end is a rising society struggling to reach a common goal, and at the other end is the individual decline of ethics and social standards.

Trier's history paints a vivid chronicle of broken walls. During the Second World War, the German army fought like lions to defend their walls and borders from advancing Allies. Their walls did not stop the overpowering forces that landed on the beaches of Normandy to liberate Europe. These forces advanced on German borders. Artillery and mortar fire howled as the Battle of the Bulge was fought. The beauty of Trier was dimmed by violence once again. I can almost hear echoes of the sounds and screams of these fierce battles. The scars of battle are still evident, yet there is now serenity and beauty in a city filled with people at peace.

The battle for holiness in a Remnant life is similar to the battle history of this beautiful German town. Some of the ruins of our past may occasionally loom up before us, like the walls of the great Roman baths in Trier. But with Christ, old walls or barriers no longer hold us back; they have tumbled down.

Standing by one of these walls while waiting for a friend, I reached out to touch the rough stone that so many others had touched during the past centuries. It seemed as though I was linking myself to the fellow humans who had once stood in that spot. These walls could tell me so much if they could talk. I began to think about the hundreds of generations who had probably stopped at this wall. I was another in the continuing line of life until the return of Jesus Christ.

How many others had known and followed Jesus? What other gods had some depended upon as power grew and faded at this wall? Had there been a first-century Christian, a disciple or a teacher of the Scriptures, who had also taught His Word by this wall? Each person, with his or her own concerns, was meeting the challenges of families, work, relationships, and survival. How many, I wondered, were a part of the Remnant?

I wondered if Christians, at the time of Constantine around the year A.D. 300, had stopped to share the truth of Christ with a friend, merchant, or child at just this spot? Had Christ's Word been shared inside the wall's gardens and community baths? Had the splendor of the walls and gardens been worshipped instead of Christ?

Seasons of time may change, but life is recorded as one faces battles and walls. When I visited this ancient city so rich in history, people were still walking by the first-century walls. Their faces and lifestyles were a bit different, but yet nothing had really changed.

For years, the Barbarians were poised across the Rhine River, unable to get across. Did those who walked by this wall ever realize that the river would freeze one extreme winter and the Barbarians would cross it? As they walked by where I stood now, did they dream that the Empire would become so weakened that the Barbarians could overrun Trier and eventually Rome itself?

Perhaps during the war years of the 1940s, someone had leaned against this wall. A broken heart may have called out to the Lord for an end to the devastation and suffering. Wounded and suffering physically or spiritually, someone may have leaned against this wall in prayer and had it answered by our compassionate God.

Walls can also be a welcome protective shield. Although now Trier's city walls are breached and broken, sections still stand today in spite of all the battles that have been played out around them. It's not only a tribute to ancient skills, but a reminder that the right protective wall, the wall of God, will not crumble before the attacks of the world.

Faith is a shielding wall that protects you from fear, doubt, worry and defeat at the hands of the enemy. The ancient city of Jerusalem was surrounded by such walls. Breaking the covenant made with God resulted in broken and breached walls, and Jerusalem lost the protection of God. Obedience is the key to triumphant life. Can God trust you to keep His covenant requirements?

The beloved of God had His wall on each side of them when they crossed the Red Sea. His wall held back the water. This mighty wall of protection later surrounded Joshua and the covenant people. It held back the Jordan River, at flood stage, when the Israelites crossed to live in the Promised Land. The walls in Trier, however, no longer impeded a journey or kept people out. No longer did these walls secure those inside. Crumbling stones, lost battles, and lack of attention have left great gaps which allow free passage. Only God has power over the world's walls, and only God's formidable strength will last.

In my life, His power takes down the walls that have blinded my eyes and heart. This same power broke down the walls of the grave in a garden outside Jerusalem 2,000 years ago. Worldly power could not contain the power of God Jesus Christ in a garden grave. Worldly power could not maintain the Roman walls in Trier, Germany. Plans we build outside the will of God will crumble and fall, as they have fallen in the past.

Refusing to obey God builds a deadly wall between you and Him. These deadly walls have been built by rebellious men and women for thousands of years. Stephen, a disciple of Christ, gave us a clear warning. A man full of God's grace and power, Stephen performed great wonders as the number of followers of the resurrected and ascended Jesus Christ increased. He recalled to the members of the Freedmen Synagogue the rebellion of those who had been led out of the desert by God through Moses. He told them that Moses had told the Israelites that God had sent living words to pass on to them. Then he continued:

> But our fathers refused to obey Him. Instead, they rejected Him and in their hearts turned back to Egypt....That was the time they made an idol in the form of a calf. They brought sacrifices to it and held a celebration in honor of what their hands had made. But God turned away and gave them over to the worship of the heavenly bodies. This agrees with what is written in the book of prophets: "Did you bring Me sacrifices and offerings forty years in

the desert, O house of Israel? You have lifted up the shrine of Molech and the star of your god Rephan, the idols you made to worship. Therefore I will send you into exile" beyond Babylon. (Acts 7:39, 41–43)

We have seen that the delivered people did not leave behind the idols of Egypt. They rejected God and the person God sent to represent Him. God spoke the law to them, the law meant for a full life designed by God. Refusing to obey that law built a barren wall between man and God.

Woven through the fabric of time, the paths of Trier hold rich stories of many lives that have felt both victory and defeat. God meant for each of our lives to be woven with His special threads. A tapestry woven with the threads of our design will tear apart. Designs that hang on weak walls will not stand up under struggles and pressures. With Christ, no wall will be able to contain you or stop you. Given the challenge of tearing down a wall, Christ will be victorious.

Our walls can be built by badly chosen relationships, and crumbled and weakened by false beliefs. Christian marriages can just exist, with each partner moving no closer to the other. The walls of selfishness or anger can block hearts. Ignoring a partner can create a wall so thick that only being broken before the Lord can tear it down.

You may feel as though you continually walk into a wall when your finances just don't seem to meet the monthly bills. You see no end, no rescue. Worries, work, and just the daily routine can seem like a towering wall before you. The dreams that were so easy to dream as a child may seem so futile today.

Break through now by the power of the Holy Spirit. Your spirit must be filled with the Holy Spirit of the Triune God, so you will be empowered to live in triumph. You can triumph over all the failures of carnal man and over your past mistakes.

God has created your heart to be woven by His Son, Jesus Christ. He must be the Master, the Master Weaver of your life. Soak in His peace, His perfect peace. You are designed, I believe, to win. Your walls will not be breached, nor will your life be broken when you allow yourself to be built by Him. If God builds your life, you need not fear being breached or broken by the world.

Remnant Dependence on God

Living as a Remnant man or woman involves a two-way intimate heart relationship. From the beginning I have been amazed at how few Christians I encounter truly walk in the intimate relationship He offers through the Word and prayer. Time after time, stories of failure, god-shopping, relationship dependency, apathy, and unbelief in the personal God are shared with me.

His hand is so strong and so true, and His promises are so incredible. Men and women today are called to join God in a deeply personal relationship. They are the same as those whom God empowered and loved throughout the Old and New Testaments of the Bible.

Why were those people's lives recorded? Their history was meant to assure you and me that the unchanging God will deliver us, care for us and provide for us today. Do we need Him? Yes, indeed. Until the end of the Church Age, the return of Christ, we walk as pilgrims. We need Him in all we do.

Jesus Christ, Savior, has set His beloved free to have life— true life. *"I came that they may have life, and have it abundantly"* (John 10:10 RSV). Believe in Him, and believe He has said this to you. Ask God to give you faith if you lack it. He hears you and longs for you to talk with Him. God the Father, Son, and Holy Spirit is the only Absolute. He is Truth.

Again and again we need Him. We are designed to need His strength and wisdom. Without Him, we will struggle and falter on our earthly pilgrimage, but He is always there to rescue us, the believers. If Christ did not live, I would have given up. If Christ did not live, I could not stand the pain that exists in the fallen world around me. If Christ did not live, I would be controlled by my sins of the past and would be in bondage to my own struggle. I have learned that as I walk in the heat of earthly fires, I need to always seek the wisdom and comfort of the Master's hand.

The Refiner's Fire

He sat by a fire of sevenfold heat,
As he watched by the precious ore,
And closer he bent with a searching gaze
As he heated it more and more.
He knew he had ore that could stand the test,
And he wanted the finest gold
To mold as a crown for the King to wear,
Set with gems with a price untold.
So he laid our gold in the burning fire,
Though we fain would have said him, "nay"
And he watched the dross that we had not seen,
And it melted and passed away.
And the gold grew brighter and yet more bright;
But our eyes were so dim with tears,
We saw but the fire—not the Master's hand—
and questioned with anxious fears.
Yet our gold grew brighter and yet more bright;
As it mirrored a form above
That bent over the fire, though unseen by us,
With a look of ineffable love.
Can we think that it pleased his loving heart
to cause us a moment's pain?

Ah, no! but he saw through the present cross
The bliss of eternal gain.
So he waited there with a watchful eye,
With a love that is strong and sure,
And his gold did not suffer a bit more heat
Than was needed to make it pure.

—Author Unknown

Notes

1. Unger, *Unger's Bible Dictionary,* p. 410.
2. Vine, *Vine's Expository Dictionary,* p. 233.
3. M. Puckett, interview by author, Reno, NV, 1997. Used with permission.

Chapter 7

Who Will Be Counted His?

A relationship involves a two-way flow. Often the believer begins to receive what God offers and continues to walk with one eye on God and one on the world system. God continues to be a distant partner in life.

When you receive God's heart relationship, you will experience an outflow of love for God. You will recognize the depth of His mercy, provision and forgiveness. You will delight in God's love. You will fall in love with God the Father, Son, and Holy Spirit. You will want to return love to God in all you do.[1]

Relationship is the heart link between you and God. It involves a two-way flow of love, respect and time shared. The more important a relationship is to you, the more time you are willing to pour into it. "Well, God doesn't meet all my needs," one woman complained. This is a woman who has been fairly well provided for in life. As a matter of fact, in the global picture of food, shelter, clothing, and family, she is an extremely fortunate woman. She thinks of herself as religious, as long as that aspect of her life does not require more than a Sunday appearance at the most well-known church in town. This woman may be religious, but she is only weakly linked to God.

Do you know for yourself the truth that God has spoken? Are you counted among the foolish who, as adults, claim that you learned everything as a child in Sunday school? Have you ever matured as an adult to find the Lord your God for yourself?

No wonder so many are so willing to allow an intermediary to explain God. It is a tactic of the enemy to claim the masses. Lenin and Marx led millions to a complete rejection of the truth of God. The masses of people who refused to depend upon the faithfulness of God followed them for many years.

The socialist/communist system actually prospered only the political leaders. Rejecting God's moral truths was costly to the people of many overtaken countries. Did those who knew God fail to be witnesses to both these men who had a bitter view of Christianity?

You must be responsible for your own relationship with God. To be in relationship, you must know Him. To abdicate that responsibility to any other person is to swim in shark-infested waters. Above the surface, you may be convinced you know God through others, and yet you do not live in the truth. The dark waters beneath the surface of your life have snatched you or will snatch you into the realm of eternal death.

A missionary, a Sunday school teacher, an evangelist, a Bible study leader, or a pastor can lead you to the waters, but you must drink deeply from the only source. God's waters are restorative and refreshing, never shark-filled liar dumps.

The source of life is only Jesus Christ (John 14:6). Finding Jesus means finding the deepest, most intimate relationship of your life.

Following every command can seem to be an impossible task. We have all fallen short of the glory of God, according to the letter Paul wrote to the Romans (Romans 3:23). Remnant men and women, faithful and forgiven, are called to righteousness by God so the promises to Abraham and Moses will stand.

Life is strength when you are embraced by the grace and mercy of God. Surely, there is not a man or woman who does not seek to love and be loved. Man is created to love and be loved by God.

Glory Light

When we speak of the glory of God, we speak of the expression of His holiness.[2] Designed to be His glory while we are on earth is not just a flattering statement. It is the steadfast love of God poured out on a spouse and child. It is meeting temptations with integrity, because the Word and prayer are the food of each day:

The heavens declare the glory of God; the skies proclaim the work of His hands. (Psalm 19:1)

The flame of a brilliant torch passes from one torch to the other. A willing hand holds the torch as its radiance ignites the new torch, which is about to be carried forward. A crowd has gathered to watch the torchbearer and the passing of the flame. Their eyes sparkle radiantly. Everyone is filled with eager anticipation as the new torchbearer steps out and begins a forward journey with the glory of the flame as the focus.

The first torch carrier stands tall and strong, with the torch's flame still gloriously burning. All can see and recognize that this is a chosen light bearer who has not been deterred or run off course. The torchbearer is like the Remnant man or woman who calls God Father, having asked Jesus into his or her heart, claiming this promise:

Since you are precious and honored in My sight, and because I love you...I will...gather you....Bring My sons from afar and My daughters from the ends of the earth—everyone

who is called by My name, whom I created for My glory,
whom I formed and made.   (Isaiah 43:4–7)

So it is with those who bear the glory of God as the light of their lives, who are willing to ignite other lives out of love for God. They are radiant witnesses of His truth, easily recognized. The glory of the Lord God is borne as high as an uplifted torch, with faith and determination.

The bearer of the torch is always focused on one goal. That goal is to live a radiant life for Christ and to pass the truth to others. The bearer of the torch is a Remnant believer, and the flame is the majestic Lord God, deeply honored by the bearer.

The source of the light is truth, the Word of God Jesus Christ. John declared, *"The light shines in the darkness"* (John 1:5). Hebrews 1:3 proclaims, *"The Son is the radiance of God's glory."*

A Remnant torchbearer illuminates Jesus Christ's offer to be rescued from darkness into light. The torch holds a brilliant, burning flame that lights the way. The bearer of so great a light would never keep it hidden (Luke 11:33). He or she knows the goal is to reach another and to make the Lord's great news of new life known.

Would one who holds such a radiant light cover it or place it in a cellar? Would it be taken out once a week to be looked at for an hour and to receive a bit of light for the coming week? Many churchgoers do this.

Would the one who was so sure of his purpose hide this torch in a back room when a family member or friend was present? No, because the source of the light has great importance to both the bearer and to all who receive it and guard it.

If the light of your presence reflects the powerful presence of the Almighty God, you will not be inclined to say, "My religion is private and I keep it to myself." This statement often conveniently curtains a heart that denies the reality of the ever-present God. A Remnant believer radiates God's glory.

A Remnant believer is like an Olympic runner racing toward the prize. In Olympic track contests, you can see the runner poised in the starting blocks. The runner is focused, prepared and eager. The long-awaited athletic event has been heralded by the torchbearer. Now it becomes a matter of reaching a personal goal. At the call of the starting gun, the runner explodes from the blocks. Equipped through experience and excellent training, the runner moves forward.

The runner does not take a few backward steps or stumble to the sidelines if he is confident of victory. The Remnant runner is the Olympian. Confident, infused with the Holy Spirit, the runner is exhilarated at the prospect of victory. The race is not the time to think about one's weaknesses; it is the time to believe in one's victory.

A marvelous life is available by faith to each believer. Does your life give God glory, honor, and praise by your choices, actions, and speech? Are you eagerly running in the right lane to your greatest goal? One day a scroll will be unrolled before the heavens and the answers to these questions will be disclosed. You will be at the throne of God, and all will be revealed. Will this view be too late?

If those who bear a dim light could catch a glimpse of the future of those without true knowledge of God, I believe the world would instantly be illuminated by a fountain of His light. The glory of God cannot be contained by a willing and loving heart. God's glory will radiate from the heart.

How very opposite from the dark reflections of a lost, stubborn, or rebellious heart is the Remnant's radiant reflection. Paul's letter to the Corinthians describes a believer living for Jesus Christ:

> *Now the Lord is the Spirit, and where the Spirit of the Lord is, there is freedom. And we, who with unveiled faces all reflect the Lord's glory, are being transformed into His likeness with ever-increasing glory, which comes from the Lord.* (2 Corinthians 3:17–18)

A life surrendered to the Lord Jesus Christ results in definite changes. This is a natural flowing of new life. The Holy Spirit causes your heart to willingly yearn to do everything for the glory of God. The Holy Spirit hears your heart yearn and hears your decision to say yes! With the intercession of God Jesus Christ to become the power source, and the Holy Spirit's groaning in intercession (Romans 8:26) for the Father's will to flood your heart, mind, and soul, your life begins to glorify God.

You glorify God, not out of fear, or because of prayer requests or punishment. You glorify Him because you are willing and delight in the power of your yielded life. Experiencing His "strength beyond strength" is awesome!

Every four years throughout the world, eyes are focused on the lighting of the Olympic torch in Greece and the carrying of it to the nation that will host the great Summer Games. Nations throughout the world prepare their best and send them to the arena.

The Olympic Games, an exciting world event, was created by man and even invokes a pagan Greek god as the source of light. Nonetheless, it is an illustration of the present and future of a Remnant believer. Presently, we are being prepared for the gathering of believers, when each one will be victorious before the King. One day, all nations will be gathered into one place, drawn to the Light of Lights, Jesus Christ.

A Remnant believer both carries the flame and passes it to others, and then races on to the day of the Lord. What lamp of light do you carry? From what source do you receive the light of your own life? Your heart reflects either the glory light of God Himself or the dark glimmer of the world, the flesh, or Satan.

There is no greater glory than the glory of the Lord God. His glory has always been seen as brilliant. Ezekiel 10:4 describes the glory of the Lord as He left the idolatrous temple of Jerusalem:

> *Then the glory of the Lord rose from above the cherubim and moved to the threshold of the temple. The cloud filled the temple, and the court was full of the radiance of the glory of the Lord.*

The glory of God filled the night at the birth of Jesus Christ:

> *And there were shepherds living out in the fields nearby, keeping watch over their flocks at night. An angel of the Lord appeared to them, and the glory of the Lord shone around them.* (Luke 2:8–9)

The day is coming when the Remnant believer will personally see the magnificent sight of the New Jerusalem that was shown to the apostle John:

> *I did not see a temple in the city, because the Lord God Almighty and the Lamb are its temple. The city does not need the sun or the moon to shine on it, for the glory of God gives it light, and the Lamb is its lamp.* (Revelation 21:22–23)

Until Jesus Christ returns, the Remnant believer must carry a glory lamp that will draw others to God the Father, Son, and Holy Spirit. The reflection of God radiates from the heart and life of the believer. The plan of God will be lived out by a Remnant warrior. The torch of Christ will be borne by the faithful who have discovered God's reality within them. Why? Because as believers who walk in the forgiveness and understanding of the Lord God, they will experience God Himself within them. This experience in a heart, a mind, and a soul draws the Remnant into an intimate one-to-one relationship.

Holiness

The word *holy (Gr. hagios),* as used in 1 Peter 1:15–16, means separated from sin and consecrated to God. It also means "the state into which God's grace calls men."[3] God calls us to be holy and to be covenant believers.

Man was created in the image of God. Our "Garden of Eden sin nature means we have fallen short of that image." We have lost an essential feature of that image: holiness. God's grace (unmerited favor), exertion of our free will, and strenuous effort make holiness possible for us.[4]

God the Father, Son, and Holy Spirit has established a holy people and has directed us to that path. The blessings of God and His promises are powerful. Obedience results in God's absolute loving care and provision. The book of Deuteronomy and the books of the Old Testament or Old Covenant lead us to deeply appreciate the mercy, love and compassion of the Creator.

There is no exception. We are to be a holy people, and we have the ability to be holy through Christ. The Lord God walked and talked with the Israelites. He walks and talks with believers today. God sent the Israelites spiritual messengers, leaders, prophets, judges, and kings. We have been left with their testimony and the truth of the Old and New Testament.

Today, the written Word makes it possible for you to become a man or woman who knows God personally. You can make the choice to receive and love God. You can know His faithfulness, mercy, and love. He is as personally available to you as He was to the people of the promise. Because He is faithful, Jesus offers reconciliation to you. Holiness becomes a heart goal. New life is holy life.

Turn your heart away from Egypt, the old life, and toward the fact that God loves you enough to prove that His character has not changed throughout history.

Battle for Holiness

"I am the Lord, who makes you holy" (Exodus 31:13). Holiness *(Gr. hagiasmos)* signifies a separation to God,[5] as stated in 1 Corinthians 1:30. God calls you to Himself through Jesus Christ. Faith in Christ reconciles you to God, the Father, Son and Holy Spirit. You become righteous, a Remnant of God in a world racing toward His return. You, through belief in Jesus Christ, become redeemed by the Lord. Being set apart for God is lived inwardly as well as outwardly:

> *But thanks be to God, who always leads us in triumphal procession in Christ and through us spreads everywhere the fragrance of the knowledge of Him. For we are to God the aroma of Christ among those who are being saved and those who are perishing.* (2 Corinthians 2:14–15)

These verses confirm the incredible fact that we have been set free from sin. We will reap the benefit that leads to holiness, which results in eternal life. Why then, do battles for holiness keep popping up in our lives? God clearly tells us that we have been set free, and He will make us holy. The battle, I believe, is actually part of the process. In triumph, we experience God's strength.

Over the past several years, especially in counseling, I have often asked individuals if they accept the fact that God imparted holiness to them when they gave their lives to Christ. The majority have responded that they did not feel it was really possible for them in particular to be holy. The Scripture must refer to someone else. Do you feel this way? Do you feel that you cannot or do not want to be holy?

Some people believe that holiness is for someone else, and even the word itself makes them feel inadequate. *"Be holy"* (1 Peter 1:16), says Almighty God, like a booming voice out of the clouds, commanding what seems impossible to many. Who, but the same serpent voice that deceived Eve in the Garden of Eden, is telling your mind that you either cannot or do not want to be holy?

However, let us examine what God said in the Bible book of 1 Peter:

> *Therefore, prepare your minds for action; be self-controlled; set your hope fully on the grace to be given you when Jesus Christ is revealed.*   (1 Peter 1:13)

> *But just as He who called you is holy, so be holy in all you do; for it is written: "Be holy, because I am holy."*
> (1 Peter 1:15–16)

Beloved reader, remember that Christ bridged the gap of separation 2,000 years ago. He has made holiness a reality, but you might battle against the truth because:

1. You do not believe God, even though you may believe in God.
2. You do not *"wholeheartedly* [obey] *the form of teaching to which you were entrusted"* (Romans 6:17).

The *"form of teaching"* is important because we are personally responsible to know God through His revealed Word. Again and again, I meet believers who have had no *"form of teaching"* from God Himself. They have very little understanding of the

Word of God. The yearning for holiness is found in a heart of faith and through personal knowledge of God. Until you personally discover the character and acts of God for yourself, you will battle holiness.

God is Absolute Holiness. You can trust He will always be faithful to the faithful Remnant. A Remnant has now been made holy through Jesus Christ. A Remnant woman or man knows God and lovingly keeps the covenant with Him.

The men and women who were delivered from the gods of Egypt and bondage were no different than a delivered man or woman today. You can reach across the Red Sea and join your hand to an Israelite. The Israelites gathered at the Jordan could feel the same excitement as you do now when you choose to also believe His promise. You can hold on to His holy promises. He will battle the forces that oppose you, and will always be triumphant.

The Spirit of Truth, the Holy Spirit, will teach you the way of God when you ask. Unfortunately, until the final judgment, the entire world system we live in is in battle with God. The battle for holiness is a battle for this lifetime because the enemy, Satan, does not want God on His throne. Satan has already lost the battle. Jesus Christ won the battle for you at the cross.

Satan is a deceiver, the enemy who attacks the spiritual realm within your mind. The battle for your holiness is being fought as a war against God. Your rejection of God's moral laws is Satan's strategy. Satan does not care about you. He is furious with God.

When you choose to believe that God desires to deprive you of pleasure or fun, it allows the enemy great power in your life. You seek a counterfeit pleasure that never satisfies your soul and spirit.

I announce to you a great joy (Luke 2:10). Holy living in relationship with our Holy God will bring you great joy. Faith in God is the source of joy (Romans 15:13)!

What an error, serving a defeated enemy. Colossians 2:15 proclaims that Jesus Christ defeated Satan. Why not live in the power of the victorious Christ? Through Him you can have peace of mind, soul, and spirit. Yield your heart and ask the Holy Spirit to teach you to love holiness, because God is holiness.

God's righteousness is made evident in the Remnant life as a natural outflow of the indwelling Holy Spirit. *"This righteousness from God comes through faith in Jesus Christ to all who believe"* (Romans 3:22).

The Scriptures say all who believe are called to holiness. Those who we might think are holy, like missionaries, ministers, or priests, are not exclusively holy people. Among them and all who believe, we find the natural man is equal in the sight of God. He has given righteousness to all who believe, yet knowing that *"all have sinned and fall short of the glory of God"* (Romans 3:23).

So we should not accept that some believers are more dedicated to God than other believers. Every person who truly believes in Jesus Christ has been given the same Spirit, the Holy Spirit. Living triumphantly is not the exception. You and I are called into a fellowship with God to walk out our lives in triumph. He wants to bless us with a triumphant life. He empowers triumphant life.

This has been made possible because the Remnant believer, counted His, has been redeemed by the great work of Christ's death. The Remnant believer receives the gift and walks out his life, allowing the Holy Spirit to release righteousness to him. The word *righteousness,* as used in the book of Romans, translates into Greek as "faithfulness." Faithfulness is readily observed in a life. The Holy Spirit witnesses through a faithful man or woman. The Scriptures tell us, *"No one will be declared righteous in His sight by observing the law....This righteousness from God comes through faith in Jesus Christ to all who believe"* (Romans 3:20, 22).

Holy People

A holy people includes all people willing to be refined and changed by God, the Father, Son, and Holy Spirit. People who are living according to the will of God are called a Remnant. Seeking, searching, and lost people will see the Remnant and know God. They will see a people who are not religious legalists.

Holy people have a heart relationship with the most magnificent, just, merciful, and awesome presence possible. The presence of God led His people out of bondage and offered them the bounty of His storehouse.

There is only one God of the Remnant. He is a God of compassion and understanding, with arms outstretched to those who do not know Him, with arms longing to surround all. He has created you and me to live as His righteous and faithful representatives to others. Holiness does not deprive you of pleasures and prosperity. Living in the will of God brings unbelievable peace. Holiness is also not an option. *"Be holy, because I am holy"* (1 Peter 1:16).

The Remnant chooses to walk in His ways. The Remnant loves God enough to be trustworthy before Him. The promises of God bring purpose, reason, and order in a world of death, pain, and confusion.

Holiness and Hope

Our natural minds tell us that the future will probably be a repeat of the past, and change is impossible. Our minds must be bound to Christ's mind. Hope and inner surety is a gift to all who know God Jesus Christ. Peter directed that you can *"prepare your minds for action,"* actions that are powered by setting *"your hope fully on the grace to be given you when Jesus Christ is revealed"* (1 Peter 1:13).

Holiness can be woven through your every action, because you believe God for every step in your life. You no longer live as a defiant child afraid of a God with a strap or switch. Now you live as a child who is affirmed, accepted, and loved by God. You find contentment and joy in obeying Him. Pleasing God out of your great love for Him is a pleasure. Hope is a gift from God.

Holiness and hope go hand-in-hand with Christ's grace and mercy. Holiness is walked out in your life as God's Remnant man or woman. Hope is life to the believer. Without hope, life is like a withered flower. With hope, the life of the Remnant believer is like a fruitful vine.

The individuals who have not walked into the kingdom by personally asking Jesus Christ into their hearts have absolutely no hope; they are *"foreigners to the covenants of the promise, without hope and without God in the world"* (Ephesians 2:12).

As a believer, the barrier or wall between God and you was destroyed by the work of Christ. The faithfulness of God and our anchor Jesus Christ guards a Remnant heart. Hope is alive for you today because Jesus Christ is alive:

> *For there is one God and one mediator between God and men, the man Christ Jesus, who gave Himself as a ransom for all men.* (1 Timothy 2:5)

Your hope can be placed completely and totally in Jesus Christ. It is futile to place your hope in yourself, family, job, friends, or material goods. As a Remnant believer on His superhighway, you can expect the blessings of God to be poured out to you. Placing your hope only in the Father, Son, and Holy Spirit means receiving God's promised blessings during your earthly pilgrimage. He offers you the hope that saves, protects, blesses, and strengthens all your relationships. He is the hope for your life journey.

Without the holiness of God, you would have to believe that life is without hope. Without hope, people perish. If you look at your child, your partner, your dreams, your business, and your work without hope, despair will fill your heart. As a young mother or father or a young person looking to find a life partner or occupational future, are you seeking to travel the highway of hopelessness? Holiness that is the natural outflow of obedience sets you on the triumphant highway.

Personal and social breakdown pave the highway of hopelessness. Stop a moment and think about where you have placed your hope in the past. How many times have you hoped for a decision or an answer to come through a human? Have you said, "I hope I can do it" when faced with a challenge, or have you known that *"I can do all things through Him who strengthens me"* (Philippians 4:13 NAS)? There is no problem too small, no dream too impossible for the Knower of your Heart.

"The world is so big and God has so much to do, He surely doesn't care about every detail of my life," someone attending one of my seminars shared. If you, too, feel this way, you have been misled. He created you to have fellowship with Him in every thought and every moment. God is omniscient. He is present 24 hours a day, 365 days a year. He never leaves or forsakes a Remnant heart (Hebrews 13:5).

For the 16 or so hours you will be awake tomorrow, talk to God throughout your day. Go directly to Him from the depths of your heart. You may be surprised at the number of hours during which you forget God in your usual schedule.

Ask the Holy Spirit to bring to your heart a desire to discover whether the Father is truly aware of all things. After all, the Word says His eye is on the sparrow, and surely His eye never leaves His own (Matthew 10:31). I believe you will be taking a Remnant step on His highway, experiencing the presence of God, battling the lies of hell's forces that deny God.

Just today I received a letter from a British couple who recently retired from a military career. They now minister to the Eastern European Military, establishing Christian fellowship. The Lord has brought us together with one heart and one mind and has even given us the opportunity to minister together. I know the following letter was sent to me by the Lord to share with you. The Lord God knows exactly what I am writing today. I believe this is a wonderful example of God's presence. This morning, I took a writing break and went to my mailbox, and here was the letter with this particular enclosure. I don't believe they enclosed such a card before. They surely are the vehicle God used to encourage you, beloved reader, so I share this with you.

Dear Friend,

How are you? I just had to send you a note to tell you how much I care about you. I saw you yesterday as you were talking with your friends; I waited all day hoping you would want to talk with me, too. I gave you a sunset to close your day and a cool breeze to rest you, and I waited.

You never came. It hurt me—but I still love you because I am your friend. I saw you sleeping last night and longed to touch your brow, so I spilled moonlight upon your face. Again I waited, wanting to rush down so we could talk. I have so many gifts for you!

You awoke and rushed off to work. My tears were in the rain. If only you would listen to me! I try to tell you in blue skies and in the quiet green grass. I whisper in the leaves on the trees and breathe in the color of the flowers;

shout it to you in the mountain streams; give the birds love songs to sing. I clothe you in warm sunshine and perfume the air with nature's scents.

My love for you is deeper than the ocean, and bigger than the biggest need in your heart! Ask me! Talk with me! Please don't forget me, I have so much to share with you! I won't trouble you any further. It is *your* decision. I have chosen you, and I still wait because I love you.

Your friend,
Jesus[6]

Remnant Lives

The testimony of the incredible courage and selflessness of Jesus Christ is an example of endurance. Because He lives within each of us, He has imparted His courage and endurance to each of us. The fact is that every believer can and should walk in that same courage, endurance, and trust.

A priest or a minister is usually perceived as living in the pursuit of holiness. "Oh, the minister is coming; let's make sure we don't argue or curse, and let's get this house cleaned up." He or she arrives, and the atmosphere changes in the room, with some feeling most uncomfortable that their usual lifestyle might be exposed in the presence of a person who seeks God. This scene, if played out in homes and gatherings, means change is necessary. Our lives should be the same with our families, friends, and all who love the Triune God. Our lifestyle should be the same at home, at work, and with all people.

God has imparted the righteousness of Christ into each surrendered life. A surrendered life, a Remnant life, is in one spirit and one heart with anyone in whom the Savior lives. Remnant hearts understand and love to be in the fellowship of His children. His glory on earth today is reflected in His own. How can we look forward to the comfort and wonder of His welcome in heaven if we are not comfortable in His presence today?

Our deep heart relationship with God the Father, Son, and Holy Spirit begins on the day when He, by grace, welcomes our repentant heart and fills our spirit with faith. From that moment, we live throughout eternity.

World wars gave us testimonies of great sacrifice and courage. Most of us deeply admire the many who endured with courage. Courage and honor and sacrifice were lived out in the decisions and battles on the home front and in concentration camps.

Most of us wonder if we could ever have Christ's strength in such horrible circumstances. Early Christians faced man-eating lions in the arenas of Rome with His courage. Christians and Jews faced the horrors of Nazi Germany. When I hear someone today say, "It is time to get on with it and forget about the Jews and Germany," I shudder. Having stood at such camps and heard the silent screams of the children and the women and the men, I cannot just "get on with it."

Courage, faith in God, selflessness, and keeping God's laws should be like breath to us. When we forget this, we have not remembered history any better than the Israelites who crossed the Jordan. We are not to hate the Germans any more than we hate the present-day Romans or Egyptians. Auschwitz, Treblinka, and Dachau were repeated in the Hanoi Hilton, Vietnam, and Bosnia. Our inner cities scream in the same pain today.

Murder flows from the heart of anyone who speaks death to any race. Murder comes from the dark forces of the leader of hell. Hitler was not and will not be the only assassin. The anti-Christ, who will rule in the Great Tribulation, will surpass any hate we have heard of or seen. A true believer does not hate those who are on this earth, because God created every man.

Killing of one race does not mean you will not be the next. It would be life-changing if we could have witnessed the ravaging of women and children in the camps of Bosnia, the purges of Soviet Russia, or the destitution and ravaging by the Soviet regime in Eastern Europe following the rape of these countries by the Germans. It would be life-changing for those with God's heart. My mind and spirit would be horrified by the hardness of the hearts who would not object.

Who will be next? Who, but the Holy Spirit, holds back the racists of our own country from acting out the mind of the anti-Christ?

My own family, half English and half Irish, has suffered at the hands of prejudice. My great-grandparents were forced from their beloved land of Ireland because of starvation and persecution. Robbed of their land, they struggled for dignity but remained faithful to the Lord.

Persecuted for their faith, the English generations on my mother's side left their homes in the 1600s to settle our country. Both peoples fled the hatred of man. Both sought new life and freedom from religious intolerance. Both sides of my family were people who believed in God.

Interestingly, their following generations then spilled this same religious pride and prejudice that they had escaped from on each other. Religion became the focus and not the Lord Jesus Christ. Each culture failed to radiate God's holiness or teach God's reconciliation to the next generation.

If we target Germany or Russia or Serbia or Bosnia, we really speak of ourselves. We spill out the same hatred. If Christ is within you and me, we have acknowledged Him as Lord. He created the earth, and our purpose is to serve Him. A Remnant believer has been freed from the bondage of prejudice and hatred.

Every day a hero of the faith lives out that purpose, many in unheralded ways. Every day, the same possibility of greed, idol worship, and cruelty lives in the natural man within ourselves. Every day, we could easily become an ancient Egyptian, whipping Israelite slaves. We could easily become a Roman guard slicing the flesh of Jesus Christ with a whip, and as easily become an SS officer beating a starving prisoner. So do not speak as I used to, "How could they?" Know beloved, life has not changed since the Garden. Man in the flesh can and will destroy. The grace of God has spared us and our country, but are we losing that grace? Our children are dying in the streets, disease is ravaging many of our young adults, and drugs are destroying all ages. The Hitler of today has many faces. The Remnant must stand for God. The Remnant must love as God loves. Personally, I have been blessed to know many who have stood and many who stand today. We can be strengthened by the power of God that is lived out in a life.

One such story is about a Remnant man who chose to minister and walk in heart relationship with God.

The Volunteer at Auschwitz
by Chuck Colson

Between 1940 and 1945, as many as two million people were murdered at the Nazi concentration camps at Auschwitz and the neighboring extermination site of Treblinka in south-central Poland. Countless acts of courage and faith took place amid the horror there. This is the story of one of them.

Maximilian Kolbe was forty-five years old in the early autumn of 1939 when the Nazis invaded his homeland. He was a Polish friar in Niepokalanow, a village near Warsaw. There, 762 priests and lay brothers lived in the largest friary in the world. Father Kolbe presided over

Niepokalanow with a combination of industry, joy, love, and humor that made him beloved by the plainspoken brethren there.

In his simple room, he sat each morning at a pigeon-hole desk, a large globe before him, praying over the world. He did so, tortured by the fact that a pale man with arresting blue eyes and a terrifying power of manipulation had whipped the people of Germany into a frenzy. Whole nations had already fallen to the evil Adolph Hitler and his Nazis.

"An atrocious conflict is brewing," Father Kolbe told a group of friars one day after he had finished prayers. "We do not know what will develop. In our beloved Poland, we must expect the worst." Father Kolbe was right. His country was next.

On September 1, 1939, the Nazi blitzkrieg broke over Poland. After several weeks, a group of Germans arrived at Niepokalanow on motorcycles and arrested Father Kolbe and all but two of his friars who had remained behind. They were loaded on trucks, then into livestock wagons, and two days later arrived at Amtitz, a prison camp.

Conditions were horrible, but not horrific. Prisoners were hungry, but no one died of starvation. Strangely, within a few weeks the brothers were released from prison. Back at the friary, they found the buildings vandalized and the Nazis in control, using the facility as a deportation camp for political prisoners, refugees and Jews.

The situation was an opportunity for ministry, and Father Kolbe took advantage of it, helping the sick and comforting the fearful.

While Kolbe and the friars used their time to serve others, the Nazis used theirs to decide just how to impose their will on the rest of Europe. To Adolph Hitler, the Jews and Slavic people were the Untermenschen (sub-humans). Their cultures and cities were to be erased and their industry appropriated for Germany. On October 2,

Hitler outlined a secret memorandum to Hans Frank, the governor general of Poland. In a few phrases he determined the grim outcome for millions: "The [ordinary] Poles are especially born for low labor...the Polish gentry must cease to exist...all representatives of the Polish intelligentsia are to be exterminated...There should be one master for the Poles, the German."

As for Poland's hundreds of thousands of priests?

"They will preach what we want them to preach," said Hitler's memo. "If any priest acts differently, we will make short work of him. The task of the priest is to keep the Poles quiet, stupid, and dull-witted."

Maximilian Kolbe was clearly a priest who "acted differently" from the Nazi's designs.

In early February 1941, the Polish underground smuggled word to Kolbe that his name was on a Gestapo list: he was about to be arrested. Kolbe knew what happened to loved ones of those who tried to elude the Nazis' grasp; their friends and colleagues were taken instead. He had no wife or children; his church was his family. And he could not risk the loss of any of his brothers in Christ. So he stayed at Niepokalanow.

At nine o'clock on the morning of February 17, Father Kolbe was sitting at his pigeonhole desk, his eyes and prayers on the globe before him, when he heard the sound of heavy vehicles outside the thick panes of his green-painted windows. He knew it was the Nazis, but he remained at his desk. He would wait for them to come to him.

After being held in Nazi prisons for several months, Father Kolbe was found guilty of the crime of publishing unapproved materials and sentenced to Auschwitz. Upon his arrival at the camp in May 1941, an SS officer informed him that the life expectancy of priests there was about a month. Kolbe was assigned to the timber detail; he was to carry felled tree trunks from one place to another. Guards stood by to ensure that the exhausted prisoners did so at a quick trot.

Years of slim rations and overwork at Niepokalanow had already weakened Kolbe. Now, under a load of wood, he staggered and collapsed. Officers converged on him, kicking him with their shiny leather boots and beating him with their whips. He was stretched out on a pile of wood, dealt fifty lashes, then shoved into a ditch, covered with branches, and left for dead.

Later, having been picked up by some brave prisoners, he awoke in a camp hospital bed alongside several other near-dead inmates. There, miraculously, he revived.

"No need to waste gas or a bullet on that one," chuckled one SS officer to another. "He'll be dead soon."

Kolbe was switched to other work and transferred to Barracks 14, where he continued to minister to his fellow prisoners, so tortured by hunger they could not sleep.

By the end of July 1941, Auschwitz was working like a well-organized killing machine, and the Nazis congratulated themselves on their efficiency. The camp's five chimneys never stopped smoking. The stench was terrible, but the results were excellent: eight thousand Jews could be stripped, their possessions appropriated for the Reich, gassed, and cremated—all in twenty-four hours. Every twenty-four hours.

About the only problem was the occasional prisoner from the work side of the camp who would figure out a way to escape. When these escapees were caught, as they usually were, they would be hanged with special nooses that slowly choked out their miserable lives—a grave warning to others who might be tempted to try.

Then one July night as the frogs and insects in the marshy land surrounding the camp began their evening chorus, the air was suddenly filled with the baying of dogs, the curses of the soldiers, and the roar of motorcycles. A man had escaped from Barracks 14.

The next morning there was a peculiar tension as the ranks of phantom-thin prisoners lined up for morning roll call in the central square, their eyes on the large gallows before them. But there was no condemned man standing there, his hands bound behind him, his face bloodied from blows and dog bites. That meant the prisoner had made it out of Auschwitz. And that meant death for some of those who remained.

After the roll call, Camp Commandant Fritsch ordered the dismissal of all but Barracks 14. While the rest of the camp went about its duties, the prisoners from Barracks 14 stood motionless in line. They waited, hours passed. The summer sun beat down. Some fainted and were dragged away. Some swayed in place but held on; those the SS officers beat with the butts of their guns. Father Kolbe, by some miracle, stayed on his feet, his posture as straight as his resolve.

By evening roll call the commandant was ready to levy sentence. The other prisoners had returned from their day of slave labor; now he could make a lesson out of the fate of this miserable barracks.

Fritsch began to speak, the veins in his thick neck standing out with rage. "The fugitive has not been found," he screamed. "Ten of you will die for him in the starvation bunker. Next time, twenty will be condemned."

The rows of exhausted prisoners began to sway as they heard the sentence. The guards let them; terror was part of their punishment.

The starvation bunker! Anything was better—death on the gallows, a bullet in the head at the Wall of Death, or even the gas in the chambers. All those were quick, even humane, compared to Nazi starvation, for they denied you water as well as food.

The prisoners had heard the stories from the starvation bunker in the basement of Barracks 11. They said the condemned didn't even look like human beings after a day or two. They frightened even the guards. Their throats turned to paper, their brains turned to fire, their intestines dried up and shriveled like desiccated worms.

Commandant Fritsch walked the rows of prisoners. When he stopped before a man, he would command in bad Polish, "Open your mouth! Put out your tongue! Show your teeth!" And so he went, choosing victims like horses.

His dreary assistant, Palitsch, followed behind. As Fritsch chose a man, Palitsch noted the number stamped on the prisoner's filthy shirt. The Nazis, as always, were methodical. Soon there were ten men—ten numbers neatly listed on the death roll. The chosen groaned, sweating with fear. "My poor wife," one man cried. "My poor children! What will they do?"

"Take off your shoes!" the commandant barked at the ten men. This was one of his rituals; they must march to their deaths barefoot. A pile of twenty wooden clogs made a small heap at the front of the grassy square.

Suddenly there was a commotion in the ranks. A prisoner had broken out of line, calling for the commandant. It was unheard of to leave the ranks, let alone address a Nazi officer; it was cause for execution.

Fritsch had his hand on his revolver, as did the officers behind him. But he broke precedent. Instead of shooting the prisoner, he shouted at him.

"Halt! What does this Polish pig want of me?"

The prisoners gasped. It was their beloved Father Kolbe, the priest who shared his last crust, who comforted the dying and nourished their souls. Not Father Kolbe! The frail priest spoke softly, even calmly, to the Nazi butcher. "I would like to die in place of one of the men you condemned."

Fritsch stared at the prisoner, No. 16670. He never considered them as individuals; they were just a gray blur. But he looked now. No. 16670 didn't appear to be insane.

"Why?" snapped the commandant.

Father Kolbe sensed the need for exacting diplomacy. The Nazis never reversed an order; so he must not seem to be asking him to do so. Kolbe knew the Nazi dictum of destruction: the weak and the elderly first. He would play on this well-ingrained principle.

"I am an old man, sir, and good for nothing. My life will serve no purpose."

His ploy triggered the response Kolbe wanted. "In whose place do you want to die?" asked Fritsch.

"For that one," Kolbe responded, pointing to the weeping prisoner who had bemoaned his wife and children.

Fritsch glanced at the weeping prisoner. He did look stronger than this tattered No. 16670 before him.

For the first and last time, the commandant looked Kolbe in the eye. "Who are you?" he asked.

The prisoner looked back at him, a strange fire in his dark eyes. "I am a priest."

"Ein Pfaffe!" the commandant snorted. He looked at his assistant and nodded. Palitsch drew a line through No. 5659 and wrote down No. 16670. Kolbe's place on the death ledger was set.

Father Kolbe bent down to take off his clogs, then joined the group to be marched to Barracks 11. As he did so, No. 5659 passed by him at a distance—and on the man's face was an expression so astonished that it had not yet become gratitude.

But Kolbe wasn't looking for gratitude. If he was to lay down his life for another, the fulfillment had to be in the act of obedience itself. The joy must be found in submitting his small will to the will of One more grand.

As the condemned men entered Barracks 11, guards roughly pushed them down the stairs to the basement.

"Remove your clothes!" shouted an officer. Christ died on the cross naked, Father Kolbe thought as he took off his pants and thin shirt. It is only fitting that I suffer as He suffered.

In the basement the ten men were herded into a dark, windowless cell.

"You will dry up like tulips," sneered one jailer. Then he swung the heavy door shut.

As the hours and days passed, however, the camp became aware of something extraordinary happening in the death cell. Past prisoners had spent their dying days howling, attacking one another, clawing the walls in a frenzy of despair.

But now, coming from the death box, those outside heard the faint sounds of singing. For this time the prisoners had a shepherd to gently lead them through the shadows of the valley of death, pointing them to the Great Shepherd. And perhaps for that reason Father Kolbe was the last to die.

On August 14, 1941, there were four prisoners still alive in the bunker, and it was needed for new occupants. A German doctor named Boch descended the steps of Barracks 11, four syringes in his hand. Several SS troopers and a prisoner named Brono Borgoweic (who survived Auschwitz) were with him—the former to observe and the latter to carry out the bodies.

When they swung the bunker door open, there, in the light of their flashlight, they saw Father Maximilian Kolbe, a living skeleton, propped against one wall. His head was inclined a bit to the left. He had the ghost of a smile on his lips and his eyes wide open, fixed on some faraway vision. He did not move.

The other three prisoners were on the floor, unconscious but alive. The doctor took care of them first: a jab of the needle into the bony left arm, the push of the piston in the syringe. It seemed a waste of the drug, but he had his orders. Then he approached No. 16670 and repeated the action.

In a moment, Father Kolbe was dead.[7]

Poured-Out Life

Father Kolbe, the circumstances, the oppressed, and the oppressor return to my thoughts time and again. This story sums up the Christ and the anti-Christ from the Garden to this moment. Without faith in God, it would have been a story of hopelessness. If this horror is continually repeated by humankind, there is no hope. Man is like the beast. The Remnant is the link to God's moral law. God will stop all this one day soon.

Father Kolbe was a covenant keeper. He knew a God of strength and eternal hope. His sacrifice, like that of Jesus, made God's love real. The SS commandant looked at the priest who volunteered and recognized Father Kolbe was not insane. I am encouraged, hopeful and more secure when I see that the Remnant remains. Even the most evil person recognizes Christ's truth in the eyes of a Remnant man or woman.

The apostle of Christ, Stephen, was stoned to death with the glory of God reflected on his face. Another apostle, Peter, it is said, asked to be crucified upside down when he was put to death for his stand for Christ.

Peter denied Jesus (John 18:17, 25, 27) and then saw the resurrected Savior. He experienced forgiveness, restoration, and the power of the Holy Spirit. Peter never denied Him again. I needed to know Peter was honest about his claims of Jesus' resurrection. Does the Word and man's response to it encourage my daily life today? Yes!

Were Father Kolbe's, Stephen's, or Peter's deaths rare testimonies of those who have a special anointing strength? Are holy men quite different from the regular Christian? No, their testimony is about individual faith. Believing God would surround them in their trials, these men were not disappointed. Men and women throughout the centuries have loved and trusted God in every circumstance, and God has not failed one of them. These men and women were faced with the same choices you and I have had to face.

What makes a man or woman stand on either side of a moral choice? Father Kolbe's story is vitally important to you and me.

We are the prisoners, the guards, the commandants, and the priest. Who would you choose to be in that situation?

How Satan must have howled with delight at the suffering of Father Kolbe, because God's heart was broken again, just as that day on Calvary. Now, fifty years after the fall of the Nazis, we see that God did not allow the evil ones to continue, but the same evil has surfaced again and again.

Father Kolbe's story is touching, strengthening, and heart-breaking at the same time. Would you stand as tall if you were in a prison line? Would you exchange your comfort, food, and health for another? Beloved reader, do you not see? In a momentary twist of circumstances, you could be in these situations. Do you believe that God will surround you, protect you, and empower you to endure all things? Would you yield to the short-term and join the rebellious who deny the true God?

The Remnant will stand, the Remnant will grow. The Remnant will pray for others and act on behalf of others. The Remnant believer will also comfort the dying and nourish the souls of the oppressed.

Jesus Christ saw the weeping hearts of the lost and the oppression of God's people. He was God's heart in the flesh. Christian man or woman, do you weep for the lost? You and I must!

Father Kolbe saw the weeping prisoner condemned to death. Do you see the weeping prisoner in yourself? Do you see this spiritually in the lives of your family, neighbors, fellow workers, the nation, and the world? You and I must!

If you cannot see, you hold the gun and whip of the SS officer. A Christian may fumble about and occasionally slide down a slippery slope, but the Cross convicts. The Holy Spirit will not allow a Remnant believer's heart to be cold. A Remnant wants to pour out his or her life for one reason. It is God's will!

Your life can make a great difference in even one other life. One weeping prisoner of the flesh, the world or the enemy can be set free because you poured out love in action.

> Find God...find yourself!
> Know God...know life!
> Know God...live life!

Can one person's life really influence others to want to live a Remnant life? Truly, God has commanded His own to be lights in this world. I have met many believers who have strengthened my faith, because they were steadfast in the midst of the pressures of the world. These are the Remnant lives. We all should encourage and thank the Lord for their obedience.

Is it possible to work in the competitive business world today and live for God? Offering one's life as an act of visible worship is the Remnant believer's choice. Are Remnant men or women tempted? Certainly, and the deceiver tries to sneak in attacks. Over the past years in ministry and certainly before that, I have observed those who claim to be Christians carefully. Claiming and walking can be on opposite ends.

How is it that some men choose to live in the strength of the Lord, especially men who have been successful, men who could succeed in any arena? I always look for an answer to this question, because I have seen so many men build their lives on self and idols. These men are chasing after the wind. As Solomon discovered:

> *I have seen all the works which have been done under the sun, and behold, all is vanity and striving after wind.*
> (Ecclesiastes 1:14 NAS)

One such man could be a next door neighbor, friend, fellow worker, or family member. It is in the pressures and struggles that the reality of our faith is witnessed. Obedience is witnessed as belief in God's power when circumstances are most difficult.

Doug is a man who loves God and is a covenant keeper. A husband and father of four, he faces all the struggles and pressures of a man trying to keep up with today's demands. This man loves and leads his family. He welcomes his brothers and sisters in Christ with great compassion and serves the Lord God with his whole heart.

Believers and unbelievers desperately need the witness of a man of God standing steadfast in the midst of business achievements, demanding time schedules, and a personal life. So I asked this man, Doug, about his relationship with the Lord.

God is the first priority in his life. One of the blessings of Doug's love of the Lord is that God's love flows into his marriage. Doug shared, "Selfishness and selfish love yields to God. We have a greater, more solid love and affection toward each other day after day."

Doug walks as the spiritual head of his home. His wife and his family are walking with him. A wife without a husband who prays, reads the Word, and models the Father's heart toward her is never at peace, never comforted. Men and women of the world need to see His plan walked out in parenting and partnerships. A Remnant man secures his wife in love just as the Father secures her husband. God has blessed this man Doug, and he brings blessings to the family.

Describing how the Word of God has changed his life, Doug said he has full confidence in his relationship with God. He knows God as Father, Jesus as his Savior, and the Holy Spirit as his comforter, teacher, and friend. In addition to God's Word, prayer is the other ingredient of a Remnant life, and Doug lives a life of continual prayer alone and with his family and other believers.

Knowing God has given Doug a love for the Lord that keeps him faithful to the will of God. "Then," he says, "it's not an effort, it's a pleasure." This is a bottom-line truth when living triumphantly as a Remnant man or woman. Remaining faithful to God is a pleasure! Truth that is known in the heart is lived out in a life.

Observing the day-to-day life of Doug has been a blessing to me. Jesus Christ was a man of strength, wisdom and faithfulness to God. Insecure men chase the world's dreams for satisfaction, and often I hear that business and Jesus don't mix in the real world. So when believers and unbelievers can actually see a man who is a successful businessman loving God and his family, it is a marvelous testimony to the Lord.

A godly man who walks a true walk builds the body of Christ. Men who are in personal bondage or who neglect their families or who give into compulsive behavior are never seen as living in triumph. Knowing such men will discourage believers and turn away the unbeliever. When I have the opportunity to observe a life over a period of time and find a Remnant disciple, I am overjoyed. God knew none of us would walk in perfection, but we can walk in triumph.

How did Doug, a man with many talents and options, choose to live in Christ, the most significant life? He was willing to share his story with you if it would give God the glory. "In my early thirties, I finally decided to find out the truth about God and Jesus Christ. My search for the truth was answered on March 21, 1982. While driving my car on my way to work, God made His presence known to me. My eyes were opened. Life took on a new meaning. Life became amazing and astonishing, taking on a true purpose—an eternal purpose.

"Anxieties and selfishness gave way and are continuing to give way to peace and confidence through Christ. This, I know, came from God. I have a greater interest and love toward others and no fear of giving away things where there is a need. More recently, I have come to realize that we have been living far below where God wants us to live. So much has been stolen from man. We should and can have it all back through Jesus Christ and the knowledge of His truth."

Surely, the tempter, the deceiver, must throw all sorts of temptations at men like Doug. How does he triumph in these situations?

Recognizing sexual and ethical situations that are not from God is important. They do arise. "I face them squarely to deal with them. I repent and receive God's forgiveness. The most difficult situations I face are giving into more 'acceptable' situations like illness or financial pressure. I know now the temptation is to give in rather than to stand on God's Word. His Word, His promises, give me authority, in the name of Jesus, and dominion over these attacks."

In summary, how does Doug live in triumph, growing in the ways of God? This brother lives and models what he speaks. "I know that the situation and key to success and victory in all these areas where difficult decisions arise is to go deep into God and His Word and through the Blood of the Lamb."[8]

Notes

1. P. D. Fritz, *The Next Step: Cultivating and Encouraging* (Bible Study) (Reno, NV: Crowne Emerald Publishers, 1996), p. 9.

2. Unger, *Unger's Bible Dictionary,* p. 409.

3. Vine, *Vine's Expository Dictionary,* p. 226.

4. Unger, *Unger's Bible Dictionary,* p. 495.

5. Vine, *Vine's Expository Dictionary,* p. 225.

6. Kevin Mayhem. Source unknown.

7. Chuck Colson, *The Body* (Nashville: Word Publishers, 1992). All rights reserved.

8. Doug Venn, interview by author, Ireland/Canada, 1996. Used with permission.

Chapter 8

The Church

The word *church (Gr. ekklesia)* has at least five meanings, according to Unger:

1. The entire body of those who are savingly related to Christ.
2. A particular Christian denomination.
3. The aggregate of all the ecclesiastical communions professing faith in Christ.
4. A single organized Christian group.
5. A building designated for Christian worship.[1]

In discussing the church in this section, I am primarily referring to points two through five above.

Today the 20th century church and its leaders need a covenant renewal. Are many of those claiming to be God's Church today more comfortable with the practices of King Saul or King Manasseh? God's Church, the bride of Christ, includes those who are obedient to Him, bowing only to His sovereignty. The church as a group or an institution or a building needs constant inspection.

God's Church is a challenged church today. Within a small city or town, there can be hundreds of churches of many denominations. If there are so many churches, why are so few committed to Christ? Why are so few reaching out to others for Christ? Do the flock within a church truly know God because they have experienced Him?

Throughout the nations, I have worshipped with gatherings of people in many churches. I have attended scores of churches throughout the U.S. as a visitor or speaker. Many of those people will certainly be counted as Remnant believers. These gatherings can be defined as particular organized groups or denominations. Many are alive and faithful churches, true spiritual centers. But I am alarmed by those that are spiritually dead. I am alarmed by the members of churches who have bowed to man's gods.

Also we must question, is all well with the soul of America's churches?

Author and Pastor Tony Evans stated that the church has fallen short because of deep spiritual problems. He wrote that the problems plaguing the church today have a perfect parallel to the circumstances in ancient Israel,[2] described in the following:

> *For a long time Israel was without the true God, without a priest to teach and without the law. In those days it was not safe to travel about, for all the inhabitants of the lands were in great turmoil. One nation was being crushed by another and one city by another, because God was troubling them with every kind of distress.*
>
> (2 Chronicles 15:3, 5–6)

Dr. Tony Evans wrote, "One of the primary things weakening America is the weakness of the church." As in the Promised Land, those who may be claiming to lead the church have man-designed religions and many may not be placing God, the Father and His Son, Jesus Christ, first. All believers, when equipped in the Word, should be able to test every pastor, priest or leader. God knew there would be false teachers and false prophets; there always have been. He has given us the truth through His Word and through a personal relationship with Him. Not allowing any false shepherd to lead the young in Christ astray is the Remnant's responsibility. We must all become disciples of God Himself.

Evans continues, "Where are the people whose lives are centered on God's Word, who live for His glory, and whose commitment it is to carry out His program? Where are the people who are willing to surrender their existence to the will of God, no matter what the price, because they are here?"[3]

As the Remnant, we are to surrender all of our own will to the Lord's, so we can become one with the Church, the bride of Christ. A believer is the Church. No institution, no religion, no human is the head of the Savior's Church. God will not allow it. He equally loves each precious heart within His Church. He loves the believers so deeply that He calls us His bride.

The church should be meeting the needs of the lost, the hungry, the hurting, and all those to whom Jesus opens His arms. There are many small, poor churches that are the glory of the Lord because of their righteousness and ministry.

I have sat in churches that appoint people to leadership who are destined to destroy the flock. Churches excuse sin in their leaders who seek personal glory. At times, this may be a product of men or women who have good intentions, but they have not been called by God to shepherd. Self-appointed or appointed leader's homes are not in order. Personal prayer, worship, and intimacy with God are lacking in false leaders. If bad yeast is allowed in a church, it will spread throughout. The result is unhealed, hurting people within that church.

Some of these churches, filled with attendees who earn good incomes, do not tend to the widow, orphan, and alien. These churches build unto themselves and have fine-looking programs. These churches publicize their works and have a sleek-appearing system. However, the spirit that prevails is not the Holy Spirit. There is little difference between a community charitable organization and the temple of God.

Many within, approved by weak leaders, lead Bible studies and do charitable works, but lead rebellious private lives. The shepherd of that church experiences struggle and failure. He or she is ultimately accountable to God. I wonder how many realize that such things will burn as stubble before the throne of God. Often this is the willfulness of Adam and Eve and the willfulness of the Israelites being repeated, living just a heartbeat away from destruction by a holy God.

God is not our servant; the Remnant is the servant of God and is called a friend of God. The Church must be holy so it will glorify God. Being a friend of God is an honor, not an automatic delivery. He is holy, majestic, and just, and He is to be reverenced.

A true Church of God is alive and draws the lost to Christ. Pastoral care is given to meet the needs of the flock. Leadership should work to disciple every man, woman, and child so they know and love the Father, Son, and Holy Spirit. If the Holy Spirit is not present, there is the danger that the gatherings in today's churches are nothing more than a vain attempt at group therapy.

A church must be a place of worship and holiness. A shepherd should know his sheep, just like Jesus knows every one. The shepherd will pick up and carry those who stumble or who do not really know God. As the shepherd of a flock of sheep did in ancient times and still does today, a man or woman called by God carries the weaker sheep close to his heart, under his cloak, so the young one is comforted.

The Church, the bride of Christ, and the Remnant must grow and mature. The Remnant is responsible to walk in the footsteps of Christ. I have encountered believers who think the church is a feeding trough. Regular church attendance is not enough. The pastor teaches, feeds, loves, and encourages each within the flock. His focus is the community where God has placed him. The Remnant is to be as Christ, going out into the world as His glory, feeding others, not seeking personal satisfaction or performing so God will reward them.

I praise God for the shepherd and sheep who live the Remnant life. They are healed and are at peace with God, building the body and reaching out for Him. God has appointed many today who are living in obedience and following Him. Gathered across this country and the world in weekly worship, praise and learning, are millions of His beloved. They are living in triumph as Remnant believers, believers in an intimate relationship with Almighty God. What joy it is for Remnant believers to be with each other today, and how very much they need it. Churches should gather to be mutually helpful to each other and to promote the glory of God.

Billy Graham, in an issue of *Decision Magazine*, recognized, "You can attend church, you can claim to be a Christian, but still not know Jesus Christ."[4] Many churches are not establishing people in covenant relationship with God. Churches should be filled with the Remnant. The Remnant should be learning and sharing God and His Word with others.

The Lord has sent me to many nations and to many people. Often, I am asked how this happened. Discipleship and Evangelism WorldWide originated and grew through the Father's call and Holy Spirit's leading. Jesus Christ's love and reality are the foundation stone. His command to *"go and make disciples...teaching them"* (Matthew 28:19–20) struck my heart.

I began to look at people who were hurting, seeking, and being complacent about God. The Lord seemed to be showing me then, as He still does now, that churches were not placing Him first, and were standing between Him and His beloved. People were being told about Jesus but were still wandering in the wilderness. Churches became a platform, a place to meet the needs of the "me first."

Bulls and Blue Jays

Expecting that those who had gone to a Christian church longer than I had or who were more familiar with the Bible would be steadfast in their walk, I had much to learn. I trusted believers to be accountable to God for how they acted toward the poor, the alien, and the widow. That is what God commanded. I experienced many who did and many who acted in anger like trapped bulls. Others behaved like shrill blue jays, screeching because they could not have their way.

The bulls and the blue jays are the most wearying. I finally recognized that the problem was that bulls and blue jays are destroyers and distracters that do not come from the Lord God. They try to weary people who follow God or who are wholeheartedly serving the Lord.

He has given me specific directions for D.E.W.W. Ministry. The Lord has kept it alive and always changing, which is the natural result of growth. God is a God of growth. He has built the team, not me. I have been charged to discern whom He called to do this particular work and whom He did not call. Each step of change has been reached when I have learned what He wanted me to learn the step before. What an incredible journey it has been! One of the difficult challenges has been to not allow a shrieking blue jay or a charging bull to stop His work.

The process of growth and development within me is continuous. I hit a wall every so often, because I fail to open my eyes and ears to see His open door. God has opened doors for incredible opportunities to spread the Gospel and the Word through D.E.W.W. Ministry. He has also allowed me to encounter some difficult people. He has caused me to want everyone else to know how free life is in His strength. His wisdom has been poured out.

We live in the promise that God will shield us. He has shielded me with His great protection, I do know that. I find it very hard to share the difficult parts of my life, because God has filled my life with the greatest of joys, the most wonderful relationships and the benefits of being a child of His promise. I share the painful times and struggles so you will know that defeat is not the nature of God. Trusting a mighty Savior to heal wounds brings peace in every circumstance. Having the moral law of God to both correct and assure me is powerful.

My life is a testimony to the promise of Jesus, "Priscilla, I have come to give you life and life abundant." (See John 10:10.) Never think He will do any less in your life, if you believe.

Living in triumph is not just an encouraging idea. My God makes it possible for me to live triumphantly. My God is one with whom I discuss everything. My God paves the way before me. My God gives me the desires and the delights of my heart. My God fights my battles, changes my circumstances and opens amazing doors.

When I encounter a person who shrieks like a blue jay, my gracious Father shows me his or her agenda and expectations. Blue jays no longer interrupt songbirds, and bulls no longer overrun the lambs that God puts alongside of me. Part of the walk in the fallen world is to encounter both blue jays and bulls.

Jesus was spit upon and crucified; should I not be challenged through my disappointments with people? In my lifetime, I am sure I have disappointed many as well. Saved by His grace and growing in His image, I am ultimately responsible to God. I choose to obey Him and allow Him to carry out His will for me.

Actually, it is counter-productive to dwell on those who tear His work down. It is much more important to focus on the many people who want to build His kingdom and do His work. Praise God for all the servants who place Him first. I thank the Holy Spirit who allows me to find them throughout the world.

Satan would love to distract us and tie us up with people who throw hooks into our minds and drag along behind us saying, "Go this way. Go that way. I don't want to follow, I want to lead." Bulls and blue jays distract our minds and waste energy.

My heart does feel sorrow for those who stay on a bull or blue jay treadmill. I choose to give them to God who will discipline or heal them. My heart is always broken for those who are in pain, lost, confused, abused and bowing down to the world, flesh or enemy.

You, too, have a special purpose that comes from the Lord if you walk with Him. Listen to Him, not others, as to how your energy, time, and resources should be spent. They are all His. If your ear is filled with the noises of the bulls or blue jays, you will struggle in your own wisdom and miss the intimacy of hearing the gentle whispers of God.

The Lord told the prophet Elijah to go stand by himself on a mountain, Horeb, in the middle of the desert. God told Elijah that the presence of the Lord would show up:

Then a great and powerful wind tore the mountains apart and shattered the rocks before the Lord, but the Lord was not in the wind. After the wind there was an earthquake, but the Lord was not in the earthquake. After the earthquake came a fire, but the Lord was not in the fire. And after the fire came a gentle whisper. When Elijah heard it, he pulled his cloak over his face and went out and stood at the mouth of the cave. Then a voice said to him, "What are you doing here, Elijah?"   (1 Kings 19:11–13)

Today He wants to talk with you, and He will when you are alone during a desert experience. Being alone with God does not mean sitting in an empty space. Call out to Him for His presence to heal you.

I had so much training academically that I had to learn to deeply seek His presence in ministry. I tried to gather a team on my own. How I had underestimated my God who, once I understood enough to get alone with Him, had excellent people in the wings waiting to do what He had called them to do. No longer do I have to manage every detail. His Remnant, with selfless hearts, work on a team dedicated to Him. The results are more powerful than the human mind can imagine. There are no bulls or blue jays to distract us from the hard work and sacrificial hours we lovingly give to Him. All is given to Him with thankful hearts; there are so many willing to do this.

All of us could accomplish much in the world's way, no doubt. Look at the world's excellent workers and planners. From all walks of life and all levels of education and income, excellent and productive people are among us.

The problem is without Jesus Christ's reconciliation of each individual to the Father, a life is like a ship in a bottle. Never will it reach full sail and voyage beyond its glass walls. The water and the wind are missing for the bottled boat and for the helmsman. The man or woman who strives for success without the true God will find in the end that life has been a confusing parable, as Jesus said to His Remnant disciples:

The secret of the kingdom of God has been given to you. But to those on the outside everything is said in parables so that, "they may be ever seeing but never perceiving, and ever hearing but never understanding; otherwise they might turn and be forgiven!" (Mark 4:11–12)

All men will meet the Savior Jesus Christ face-to-face. Some who have spent a lifetime working toward success, awards, and riches will face the moment in despair. Not one of these earthly treasures will be there with him. Each of us will encounter God alone.

Man will bring his or her temper, worship of drugs, money, alcohol, or greed to greet God and will have unending time to hate these things.

Woe to the Shepherds

Former Secretary of State Henry Kissinger once warned, "Domestic weakness encourages foreign intervention."[5] Likewise, weakness within the Christian gathering of believers opens doors to false gods, false shepherds (leaders), and compromise.

The book of Revelation warns those who, although they work hard for God, have fallen away from their first love. They have fallen into dangerous territory. *"Remember the height from which you have fallen!"* (Revelation 2:5). God commands us to listen to what the Holy Spirit is speaking to the churches.

Jesus Christ is the Shepherd of the believer and the Healer of the wounded or dying. Throughout the Word of God are stern warnings to false leaders. God knew they would harm His own. Every pastor, priest, and leader will face God and will be accountable for every one of the flock and for every word and action. False shepherds, who may first worship the numbers in the church and church buildings, weaken the body and prepare themselves for judgment.

God spoke very emphatically through the prophet Jeremiah: *"Woe to the shepherds who are destroying and scattering the sheep of My pasture!"* (Jeremiah 23:1). God judges and will judge the leaders of the churches who are not taking care of His Remnant. The Remnant need not fear this judgment, because the leaders are held responsible. Jesus Christ came and is our True Shepherd. His final return will mean the end of false leaders and the end of false churches. There is one Church, and that is the body of the Remnant.

God warns religious leaders, *"'Because you have scattered My flock and driven them away and have not bestowed care on them, I will bestow punishment on you for the evil you have done,' declares the Lord"* (Jeremiah 23:2).

Pastors and leaders of churches have sometimes placed the buildings, the numbers, and personal recognition above time spent with people. Some large churches have pastors with no other personal touch except to stand above the flock once or twice a week. Other churches have performers in the pulpit who neglect their wives, husbands, and children at home.

When God appoints and anoints a shepherd of His flock, the shepherd or pastor should not design his or her own role. Certainly, God's people look for the pastor, priest, or minister to reflect the heart and actions of Jesus Christ. God's anger toward the rebellious religious leaders of ancient Israel should cause anyone who stands as a shepherd to honor God's command.

Speaking through the prophet Ezekiel, God required a shepherd to care for His flock in the following ways:

1. Strengthen the weak.
2. Heal the sick.
3. Bind up the injured.
4. Bring back the strays.
5. Search for the lost.

Ezekiel 34:4

Are the churches of America and the world placing the weak, sick, injured, strayed, or lost in a safe and loving pasture? More and more, the God of the Bible has been diluted and compromised. The beloved sheep of His flock find a pasture in which people are still weak, sick, injured, straying, and lost.

God holds any pastor, priest, or minister responsible. God says in Ezekiel 34:10 that He will hold His shepherds responsible for His flock. If a shepherd is God-appointed, then God's people find healing and new life.

The churches are not radiating the healing touch of God through the people. Why in any given city in America and in many other countries are the churches not filled with worshipful disciples who are gathered together to love the True Shepherd, Jesus Christ? The false shepherds of today who gather people together by the millions are gathering seekers. These seekers are not finding the truth in lukewarm, compromising, or separatist churches. Cults grow because they counterfeit Christ. Man has designed religions and contemporary gods from the beginning and is still doing the same today.

Are there many of your neighbors, workmates, family, friends, or acquaintances who testify that the Christian church is more fulfilling to them than a popular movie, theme park, sporting event, or concert? The Remnant of God has to become a warrior for the Lord. Praise God that His Remnant people can recognize the liar by the Holy Spirit's gift of discernment.

I praise God that I have met time and time again the most incredible co-laborers for the Gospel—rich, poor, shepherds, flocks and sisters and brothers who keep the Covenant. God, through Jeremiah, promised,

> *I Myself will gather the Remnant of My flock out of all the countries where I have driven them and will bring them back to their pasture, where they will be fruitful and*

increase in number. I will place shepherds over them who
will tend them. (Jeremiah 23:3–4)

I am nourished, encouraged, comforted, and restful in the presence of the Remnant. I see God reflected through them, I learn from them and I am refreshed by them, His beloved. The Holy Spirit confirms to my spirit the love they have for Him. The presence of the Lord surrounds these marvelous people of God who have blessed me—leaders of government, the military, the ministry, mothers, fathers, pastors, teachers, laborers, and servants. All are equal in God's love.

The Lord God has His warriors and servants throughout the world preaching the Gospel. They gather believers together and equip the Remnant to stand. The actual numbers of these churches are known only to Him, and the glory is given only to Him. However, churches and shepherds living in obedience to God's Word are easily known by the lives of the people within the flock.

Who would dare to stand before Almighty God and say that some of the true Christians, who have believed in Jesus Christ as Savior and Lord of their lives, will not be numbered in the Remnant? Will not human wisdom be but such a small thing in glory light? The Gospels clearly make it known that the Creator God gathers and prepares His Remnant. You and I must keep our eyes on the Son, who covers the earth with His light. Through Him, the Church lives, both the whole Remnant (the Church) and the particular groups (the churches).

God will hold accountable those in a church who deliberately and continually cause spiritual death or deceit. They will share the destiny and companionship of the liar in his lake of fire. We have a reason why God has called the Remnant to be His light on earth. The Remnant is here for His purposes. They are to make known the truth that one can be reconciled to the Father by a personal decision to yield one's life to Him through God Jesus Christ. *"I am the way and the truth and the life. No one comes to the Father except through Me."* This was spoken by the Savior in John 14:6.

The Remnant, in the midst of the swirling mirrors and lights of deception, knows and follows the will of God. The Remnant is called out to witness to the truth of the Word and God the Father, Son, and Holy Spirit. This is the Church! But look how man has tried to package it since the first-century disciples gathered in fellowship.

Often, groups of people declare themselves the only real Church. This control comes from fear or greed and must be brought before the throne of God to be washed in His light. Groups claiming to be the select "church group" offer a plastic gospel which lures the seeking, the lonely, the unknowing, and the fast grabbers. God will not have a welcome sign for every religion. God is in relationship with each believer.

There are many false lures hanging from tantalizing fishing lines, snaring humans into spiritual death. When a fish bites a lure, it thinks it has found nourishment in its pond, lake, river, or ocean. Deceived, it is taken in by the fake bait. The fish, lifted out of its living water, cannot survive.

The best fishing lures, interestingly, are those which appear to be as close to the real thing as possible. The lures of the spiritists, mystics, psychics, cults, and mind scientists today will include the use of a retooled Jesus. Jesus will be referred to as a great man, a prophet, or God's Son, but not God the Son.

You and I must seek Him personally. We are responsible for our relationship with Him. Someone else is not. Danger, fishermen with plastic lures! We will never see the warning signs unless we go, ourselves, to Christ in prayer and to His Word.

Crowds still gather to, in effect, crucify the Savior and to thrust a spear into the side of Christ and into the heart of the

Father. Crowds still gather to wound Jesus Christ. What crowds? A crowd of a cult, a crowd of false teachers, a crowd of agnostics, a crowd of religionists. A crowd of violent gangs, liars, cheats, and "good people" who insist upon the standards of their own god. A crowd of those who have stood on the shores of the symbolic Jordan and crossed into idolatry. A crowd of astrologers who chart a life on the created, not the Creator. A crowd in the United States that is filled with psychics who claim to have the power to see the future. A crowd of those who seek the mind of man in those dark spirits and reject the Holy Spirit. These crowds seem endless.

The gathering of people together before God is important to Him. He met in fellowship with Adam and Eve in the Garden of Eden, and He gathered His people in Egypt and led them across the Red Sea. He walked with them as a people. He parted the sea so they could cross to a new life. God gathered His people in the desert at Sinai so He could enter into a covenant relationship with them.

When the Israelites were gathered at the Jordan River, after forty years of desert cleansing, God commanded obedience and they promised to obey Him. In return, God promised they would possess the land (Deuteronomy 4:5). He gathered them again to lead them into the land He had promised to them.

"Hear, O Israel," God called then and calls to you now. The Remnant shall be gathered to Him when the final day arrives. You can choose to live in triumph while you await that gathering:

> *When the Son of Man shall come in His glory, and all the holy angels with Him, then shall He sit upon the throne of His Glory. And before Him shall be gathered all nations: and He shall separate them one from another, as a shepherd divideth His sheep from the goats.*
>
> (Matthew 25:31–32 KJV)

This is great news that confirms the Remnant has a definite time frame on this earth. God's powerful announcement states that the world's moral circus will continue to create its own show, but only for a limited time. God plans to gather the Remnant to Himself and also to deal with blinded and darkened hearts.

It is good news for those who choose triumphant life and devastating news for those who are living in defeat. The trumpet of heaven will soon announce the true triumph. It is certain that we will know when He has returned! *"The Son of Man will come at the hour you do not expect Him"* (Matthew 24:44).

Matthew 25 tells us that God knows those who are His own sheep. We see that He will personally separate all the people, some to His right hand and some to His left. The right hand is the place of honor, as Jesus is seated at the right hand of the Father.

Who goes where? He sets the sheep on the right and the goats on the left, according to Matthew 25:34 (TLB). What happens next? *"Then I, the King, shall say to those on my right, 'Come, blessed of my Father, into the Kingdom prepared for you from the founding of the world.'"*

The King of Kings, Jesus, will gather His Remnant before Him, to worship Him and to hear from Him, according to the plan of God.

The Holy Spirit showed me that church attendees need desperately to know God, not man. Fellowship, greater numbers, and events are becoming king in our churches. Some are worshipping a particular religion or denomination before they worship the King. It happens in church on Sunday and lasts all week long. Unhealed, like sheep outside the pasture fences, people are wandering, longing for Him. Wolves, lying in wait for those who do not know that God will secure them personally, devour whoever is not protected by the shepherd. But for those who believe, God will take them into safe pasture.

Billy Graham's testimony reminds me that it is critical to have a personal relationship with God. A personal relationship with a church can leave many with troubled hearts.

> Before I received Christ as my Savior, I was a member of a church. I had been baptized. I attended church every Sunday because my parents made me. And yet inside I knew that something was wrong. I didn't have the peace and the happiness and the joy that the Bible talks about. I didn't have the absolute assurance that I was right with God. I wanted it, but I didn't know what to do. So there came a time when I got down on my knees, and I repented of my sins. I said, "O God, I'm a sinner. I'm sorry for my sin. I turn from my sin, and I turn to Christ. And I believe."[6]

Noted 17th-century philosopher Spinoza observed:

> I have often wondered that persons who make a boast of professing the Christian religion, namely, love, joy, peace, temperance and charity to all men, should quarrel with such rancorous animosity, and display daily toward one another such bitter hatred; that this, rather than the virtues they claim, is the readiest criterion of their faith.[7]

In an interview, a well-known author and minister, Frederick Buechner, said, "Today's preachers and churches often fail to be people and places that point toward home (heaven)." He continued to say that he "often leaves church feeling disappointed, even deceived."[8]

Consider the depth of the heart trust of Abraham, Joseph, and Moses in the Lord God. The integrity and wisdom of these men reflect the integrity and wisdom of God the Father, Son, and Holy Spirit. They were models for those who would be called by God Himself to be shepherds to the Remnant until the day of the Lord.

Notes

1. Unger, *Unger's Bible Dictionary,* p. 204.

2. Tony Evans, *Are Christians Destroying America?* (Chicago: Moody Press, 1996), p. 2.

3. Ibid, p. 86.

4. Billy Graham, "Certainty in a World of Change," *Decision Magazine* (October 1996): p. 2.

5. Henry Kissinger, *American Foreign Policy* (New York: W.W. Norton and Co., 1969), p. 81.

6. Graham, "World of Change," p. 3.

7. J. Adler and C. Van Doren, *The Great Treasury of Western Thought* (New York: R.R. Bowker Company, 1977), p. 1296.

8. F. Buechner, "Religion," *Publisher's Weekly Religion Bookline* (1 June 1996): p. 7.

Chapter 9

Living in Triumph

O My people, hear My
teaching; listen to the words of My mouth.
—Psalm 78:1

God, intimate and personal, calls us in Psalm 78 to remind us of His faithfulness throughout the generations. In spite of His people's rebellion, He is merciful.

Mercy *(Gr. oiktirmos)* is God's action of compassion and pity, used by God who is the "Father of mercies."[1] *"What a wonderful God we have—He is the Father of our Lord Jesus Christ, the source of every mercy, and the One who so wonderfully comforts and strengthens us in our hardships and trials"* (2 Corinthians 1:3–4 TLB).

Have you heard Him? Have you listened to what you have heard? Biblical accounts are written so that you and I can learn. Accounts of people living under the mercy of God since the beginning are written for you, so that you will be able to apply God's faithfulness to your present circumstances.

God acts according to His time line, not ours. God acts in love, mercy, and always in righteousness. He charges you and me to teach the next generation. It is His will that future generations learn from His instructions. God's interactions with His own and with those who reject the truth are life lessons that must be written on our hearts. If you are a Remnant believer, you will read and apply His words to your life with a spiritual heart.

Consider that at any time in history, Almighty God could have said, "I will destroy the earth I created because of the sin of those who refuse to be blessed." No, what He did was the following:

> *Yet He was merciful; He forgave their iniquities and did not destroy them. Time after time He restrained His anger and did not stir up His full wrath.* (Psalm 78:38)

You would not have the opportunity today to be blessed in Remnant relationship if God was not merciful. He has faithfully continued in covenant relationship with His created beings. Through the righteous Remnant, the world will know God is Truth.

Because of the Remnant (covenant keepers), He has continued in relationship with His created beings. The Bible is so very exciting, beloved reader. You can see for yourself that the grace and mercy of God have never changed. You can trust God. God clearly reveals His will and men's rebellion. Psalm 78 reminds us of His power and righteousness.

As you read Psalm 78, quiet your heart, and invite the Holy Spirit to illuminate the Word in your mind and heart. Hear God speak to you personally:

> *O my people, hear my teaching; listen to the*
> *words of my mouth.*
> *I will open my mouth in parables,*
> *I will utter hidden things, things from of old—*
> *what we have heard and known,*

202

what our fathers have told us.
We will not hide them from their children;
we will tell the next generation
the praiseworthy deeds of the Lord,
His power, and the wonders He has done.
He decreed statutes for Jacob
and established the law in Israel,
which He commanded our forefathers
to teach their children,
so the next generation would know them,
even the children yet to be born,
and they in turn would tell their children.
Then they would put their trust in God
and would not forget His deeds
but would keep His commands.
They would not be like their forefathers—
a stubborn and rebellious generation,
whose hearts were not loyal to God,
whose spirits were not faithful to Him.
The men of Ephraim, though armed with bows,
turned back on the day of battle;
they did not keep God's covenant
and refused to live by His law.
They forgot what He had done,
the wonders He had shown them.
He did miracles in the sight of their fathers
in the land of Egypt, in the region of Zoan.
He divided the sea and led them through;
He made the water stand firm like a wall.
He guided them with the cloud by day
and with light from the fire all night.
He split the rocks in the desert
and gave them water as abundant as the seas;
He brought streams out of a rocky crag
and made water flow down like rivers.
But they continued to sin against Him,

rebelling in the desert against the Most High.
They willfully put God to the test
by demanding the food they craved.
They spoke against God, saying,
"Can God spread a table in the desert?
When He struck a rock, water gushed out,
and streams flowed abundantly.
But can He also give us food?
Can He supply meat for His people?"
When the Lord heard them, He was very angry;
His fire broke out against Jacob,
and His wrath rose against Israel,
for they did not believe in God
or trust in His deliverance.
Yet He gave a command to the skies above
and opened the doors of the heavens;
He rained down manna for the people to eat,
He gave them the grain of heaven.
Men ate the bread of angels;
He sent them food they could eat.
He let loose the east wind from the heavens
and led forth the south wind by His power.
He rained meat down on them like dust,
flying birds like sand on the seashore.
He made them come down inside their camp,
all around their tents.
They ate till they had more than enough,
for He had given them what they craved.
But before they turned from the food they craved,
even while it was still in their mouths,
God's anger rose against them;
He put to death the sturdiest among them,
cutting down the young men of Israel.
In spite of all this, they kept on sinning;
in spite of His wonders, they did not believe.
So He ended their days in futility

and their years in terror.
Whenever God slew them, they would seek Him;
they eagerly turned to Him again.
They remembered that God was their Rock,
that God Most High was their Redeemer.
But then they would flatter Him with their mouths,
lying to Him with their tongues;
their hearts were not loyal to Him,
they were not faithful to His covenant.
Yet He was merciful;
He forgave their iniquities
and did not destroy them.
Time after time He restrained His anger
and did not stir up His full wrath.
He remembered that they were but flesh,
a passing breeze that does not return.
How often they rebelled against Him in the desert
and grieved Him in the wasteland!
Again and again they put God to the test;
they vexed the Holy One of Israel.
They did not remember His power—
the day He redeemed them from the oppressor,
the day He displayed His miraculous signs in Egypt,
His wonders in the region of Zoan.
He turned their rivers to blood;
they could not drink from their streams.
He sent swarms of flies that devoured them,
and frogs that devastated them.
He gave their crops to the grasshopper,
their produce to the locust.
He destroyed their vines with hail
and their sycamore-figs with sleet.
He gave over their cattle to the hail,
their livestock to bolts of lightning.
He unleashed against them His hot anger,
His wrath, indignation and hostility—
a band of destroying angels.

He prepared a path for His anger;
He did not spare them from death
but gave them over to the plague.
He struck down all the firstborn of Egypt,
the firstfruits of manhood in the tents of Ham.
But He brought His people out like a flock;
He led them like sheep through the desert.
He guided them safely, so they were unafraid;
but the sea engulfed their enemies.
Thus He brought them to the border of His holy land,
to the hill country His right hand had taken.
He drove out nations before them
and allotted their lands to them as an inheritance;
He settled the tribes of Israel in their homes.
But they put God to the test
and rebelled against the Most High;
they did not keep His statutes.
Like their fathers they were disloyal and faithless,
as unreliable as a faulty bow.
They angered Him with their high places;
they aroused His jealousy with their idols.
When God heard them, He was very angry;
He rejected Israel completely.
He abandoned the tabernacle of Shiloh,
the tent He had set up among men.
He sent the ark of His might into captivity,
His splendor into the hands of the enemy.
He gave His people over to the sword;
He was very angry with His inheritance.
Fire consumed their young men,
and their maidens had no wedding songs;
their priests were put to the sword,
and their widows could not weep.
Then the Lord awoke as from sleep,
as a man wakes from the stupor of wine.

He beat back His enemies;
He put them to everlasting shame.
Then He rejected the tents of Joseph,
He did not choose the tribe of Ephraim;
but He chose the tribe of Judah,
Mount Zion, which He loved.
He built His sanctuary like the heights,
like the earth that He established forever.
He chose David His servant
and took him from the sheep pens;
from tending the sheep He brought him
to be the shepherd of His people Jacob,
of Israel His inheritance.
And David shepherded them with integrity of heart;
with skillful hands he led them.
(Psalm 78:1–72)

Let us begin to walk triumphantly, recalling not only the ways we may have rebelled, but also recalling the blessing of believing God. *"O my people,"* how He is willing to tend you and keep you in His arms. God calls you His very own.

A Remnant believer seeks to learn and obey God's covenant commands, recalling the reality of God's promises and judgments. His Word is a clear explanation of His character and moral codes. Since the Garden of Eden, God has been in moment-by-moment relationship with His creation. You are His creation, created for moment-by-moment intimacy.

Getting What You Crave

A craving is an intense or prolonged desire, yearning, or appetite.[2] Each of us must look within ourselves to acknowledge honestly what is our most intense desire. If it is not to live in the presence of God, then we are living in defeat:

For He had given them what they craved. But before they turned from the food they craved, even while it was still in their mouths, God's anger rose against them.

(Psalm 78:29–31)

Triumphant living is the powerful experience of being in one heart and one mind with God (John 17:21). Our life choices reflect our hearts. Craving anything before God results in emptiness. We continue to strive for more, more, more of the things we crave, because our rebellious hearts refuse to repent. A relationship, food, money, power, beauty, status, and a home never satisfy without the Master.

There is no question that the social and moral structure of a people claiming to follow God will crumble when parents, families, and leaders do not obey His command to teach the following generation. Trust in God must be cultivated like a fragrant flower from seedling to bloom. Your next generation will believe what you teach if you live it.

Religion, a particular practice, does not make a Christian nor does it make a disciple. Worshipful, Christ-centered religion is certainly a part of the personal life of a Remnant believer. Remnant relationship leads to understanding God's nature. You acknowledge that the bottom line is: God is God! He does not act because we demand it. He does not give into our cravings unless it is to correct us.

This is a rather frightening thought. When we demand that God satisfy our cravings, He often will in a way we may not expect. "Do it my way," is a dangerous demand of a majestic and omniscient God. His heart and our hearts should beat securely as one. His way will satisfy.

Every so often I hear from a woman or man that she or he prayed, and God allowed living together outside of a marriage commitment. Sex apart from His law was justified because the couple would one day marry. God allows us to choose His will or our own will. The results of that choice will bring a blessing or a curse.

Usually I can hear rebellious anger in a person's voice that insists the moral laws of God do not apply to her or him in this day or time. This anger is the same angry challenge you have just read in Psalm 78:17–18: *"But they continued to sin against Him, rebelling in the desert against the Most High. They willfully put God to the test by demanding the food they craved."*

When you turn away and demand your "craving" from God, you will find that God will do just as He did thousands of years ago. He will give you what you ask for as Psalm 78:29 states, and allow the flesh to satisfy itself, if only to discipline you. The results will be the fruit of your own will. Weigh your cravings carefully against God's consequences.

However, the fact is that holy God cannot look upon sin. Separation is a high price. At first, separation and compromise may feel like a small tear in a fabric, but the result can be spiritual or even physical death. Spiritual shredding of one's life garments results, and the enemy roars with delight that another has hurt the heart of God.

God has just reason to punish rebellion with His Almighty power. He offers life, and we choose iniquity. The result for the people He brought across the Red Sea was:

1. He gave them what they craved, but the result was His anger. Punishment will come upon those who break their relationship with Him.
2. When His anger rises against rebellion, He punishes, even to death.

Trusting God results from learning how He related and responded to His people in history. We are experiencing this same

God day by day in our own lives. He disciplines for the good of His children, whom He loves intensely:

> *Then they would put their trust in God and would not forget His deeds.*   (Psalm 78:7)

Psalm 78:5–7 commands us to be witnesses to God's character by living a faithful life. Why? So that others would *"put their trust in God and would not forget His deeds."* The Remnant of the people of God have done this for thousands of years. For example, in spite of the persecution, exiles and separation of the Jews in history, they have passed their culture and identity to generation after generation.

God's Remnant have made Him known to others with each generation. That is His plan for us. The first-century disciples testified to the truth of Christ, and that testimony has given new life to generations throughout time. The Christian Remnant believer does the same today.

Be aware that the enemy of God, Satan himself, tries to imitate God. Ancient history and current events reveal that cults and false religions keep close fences around their deceived followers. There are works and performance, but there is no freedom in the cult or religion or mysticism that exalts itself. God has given us, through Psalm 78, both an explanation and historical record. We have before us the results of false worship and testing God.

Personal standards and ethics must begin within the family of each believer. New generations experience a total life change when they hear the truth. The truth is that God the Father offers steadfast love and an answer to pain, failure and confusion. Someone loved God as a Remnant believer and took the time to teach the next generation (Psalm 78:1–4). God reveals Himself through the Word; the Word of God is the key to life itself. God also reveals Himself to others through a Remnant life. A Remnant believer knows God.

When we realize that God the Son paid the price for their errors, and that God the Holy Spirit revealed the true purpose for their lives, the bondage of past generations is broken. No wonder the spirit of darkness screams in anger when a Remnant believer shares the Gospel of Jesus Christ, and a new birth is about to take place.

Larry Trammell, a gifted speaker, musician, and songwriter, is one such Remnant man, a covenant keeper. Larry experienced new life after an earnest and intense search. He called out to God, and God set him free. Larry's quest began when he started to realize that he and God were not in heart relationship, even though Larry was in active ministry. "This was when I first began to realize that someone could be full of the knowledge of the Word of God without knowing the God of the Word."[3] Larry allowed me to share one of his writings with you:

Get Ahold of Me Completely

Lord, get ahold of me completely—
    at times I've gone astray.
Oh, keep me by Your holy power within Your will, I pray.
Get ahold of me completely—
    change me, holy Lord, within
'til righteousness delights me more than all desires of sin.
Get ahold of me completely or I will surely fail.
For by myself I can't defeat the fierce onslaughts of hell.
Get ahold of me completely or I will surely fall.
I can only triumph by Your power
    which triumphs over all.
Get ahold of me completely and I'll live victoriously.
Then, not only me, but others will walk in Your liberty.
Get ahold of me completely—take filth and hypocrisy,
and in their place flood me with grace: the

power to be free.
Get ahold of me completely—
    let me not go on my own.
For without You I am nothing.
    Without You all hope is gone.
Get ahold of me completely—
    flood me with love for Your will.
Remove all hindrances within, and with Your Spirit fill.
Get ahold of me completely—
    how I long for You, my Lord.
Let me accept no less than You and I in one accord.
Get ahold of me completely—
    nothing less will ever do.
Otherwise, I'll not fulfill my call to live in love with You.
Get ahold of me completely—
    only then I'll know Your best:
knowing, serving, loving You, abiding in Your rest.[4]

Unlike Larry, some people resist change and some refuse it. Change does not take place unless it is understood and grasped in the heart. If we do not hear it and see it, we cannot understand. God's Word becomes filtered by the world, the flesh, and the enemy. The truth becomes distorted by those who refuse to be among the Remnant, those who choose to reject God's covenant offer:

> *Having the understanding darkened, being alienated from the life of God through the ignorance that is in them, because of the blindness of their heart: Who being past feeling have given themselves over unto lasciviousness, to work all uncleanness with greediness.*
>
> (Ephesians 4:18–19 KJV)

Look, also, at this word from God:

> *Let me say this, then, speaking for the Lord: Live no longer as the unsaved do, for they are blinded and confused.*

Their closed hearts are full of darkness; they are far away from the life of God because they have shut their minds against Him, and they cannot understand His ways. They don't care anymore about right and wrong and have given themselves over to impure ways. They stop at nothing, being driven by their evil minds and reckless lusts.

(Ephesians 4:17–19 TLB)

People with closed hearts are far away from the life of God and have minds shut against Him. It is easy to distinguish the Remnant from the non-Remnant among us. Non-Remnant lives begin by closing minds to His will, and then hearts fill with darkness, like slow chemical seepage into a stream. Next comes the failure to remember and trust the God of the Word. The living stream is now polluted and dying.

Find the Truth

Imagine that upon waking one morning, you discover that two newspapers have been delivered to your doorstep. The same newspaper has two different front page feature stories. One reports you are a prime suspect in a recent notorious crime. The other newspaper reports the crime and reveals the true criminal who has confessed to the wrongdoing. One headline places you under a dark shadow, while the other reveals the truth.

Which one would you hope your friends and neighbors would buy and read? Would some you know buy the wrong edition because they hoped you had actually fallen into sin? Some might want to buy the wrong edition just to feel better about their own lives of rebellion. Some might like to complain and grumble that you and everyone else are legal and moral failures these days and it is all hopeless.

A movie called *The Paper* drew my attention this past year. During a cold New England winter night, my family and I decided to gather to watch it. I rarely take time for a movie on television, but the advertised contrast of moral good versus bad ethics interested me.

Just such a plot was explored. Two headlines were being prepared about the arrest of two wrongly accused teenagers. Two editors of a newspaper were faced with the choice of printing a headline they knew was false. It would cause two young, innocent lives to be ruined by suspicion and lies. Scene after scene centered on the question of ethics. One editor pursued truth at great risk, while the other pursued a career, sensational headlines, and meeting deadlines.

Fortunately, good ethics won over greed. I was encouraged by the way it all turned out in the pursuit of truth. The presses with the wrong edition were stopped at great financial cost to the paper, and the morning headlines shouted out the innocence of the teenagers. The right way, the truth, saved the future of two young lives.

Justice is a command from God to both society and to the Remnant believer personally. Justice *(Heb. sedek)* means the outflow of God's righteousness.[5] Micah 6:8 clearly states the requirement for the Remnant today:

> *He has showed you, O man, what is good. And what does the Lord require of you? To act justly and to love mercy and to walk humbly with your God.*

The same is required in our own lives as we impact others. What is the moral code upon which you base your daily choices? These are headlines to those around you. Is it justice, mercy, and walking in the heart recognition that God is God? What has your life printed for the next generation?

The Remnant must stand in the midst of crumbling morals and values. They must have a lifestyle that stands firm for principles and values that are founded upon God's covenant with

His people. Why are there so many Christians and so few disciples? Each of us must answer that question relative to our own lives.

This Sunday paper's headlines may feature you sitting in a church, but what would it feature about you at the office? What would it feature about the movies you watch or the language you speak to others? How can the world believe God if the believer does not live in His way? Does the omnipresent God leave the church service with the pastors, musicians, ministry teams, and you and me?

Of course, I realize that as we read His Word, we see that social disorder and the crumbling of nations are not new events. Look again at Psalm 78. This is just one biblical historical outline you will find repeated over and over again throughout the centuries. God is speaking to each of His own, man or woman. He is speaking to you personally today, giving you the responsibility of teaching the new generations. It is not a command to be taken lightly.

I discovered in 1973 that God the Father, Son, and Holy Spirit made a true plan of life—and that all attempts to distort, destroy or adapt it have failed. Since then, I have always found it difficult to understand why people would want to be banished from the Garden that God created for them. The history of God's great covenant offer and the self-destruction of the people has repeated itself from creation to today.

A familiar old saying is, "Never touch a hot stove twice." After touching a hot stove once, why would we burn ourselves again and again? Our Heavenly Father has taught us personally and collectively that we will be hurt by the fires of a hot stove. Yet we race toward sin as soon as we are free to make our own choices.

Certainly, that is exactly what I did as an atheist for many years, and surely my own sin nature has drawn me to the hot stove time after time. Fortunately, the mercy of God has not allowed the fires to consume me as I have learned year after year of the peace and joy of yielding to His plan and protection. Every time I stumble, He keeps His promise to be faithful to me, as His right hand reaches down to pick me up and dust off the dirt.

Every time I am forgiven and cleansed, I realize God knows me better than I know myself. Growing and experiencing a stronger belief and trust in God in spite of my own weaknesses has been life-changing. I stand on His promise:

> *If we walk in the light, as He is in the light, we have fellowship with one another, and the blood of Jesus, His Son, purifies us from all sin.* (1 John 1:7)

> *If we confess our sins, He is faithful and just and will forgive us our sins and purify us from all unrighteousness.* (1 John 1:9)

These verses provide a life-giving promise, a release from anxiety and guilt. When we walk in the light of Christ, we confess because our hearts know we have stepped outside of His will by choice. For me, it means a desire to serve God as He directs. Believing in His forgiveness is accomplished by faith, and faith in God is a gift from Him. A ritualistic "I'm sorry," with an intent to continue, is not what God desires. It takes a heart longing for a change from the sin. Why would my heart and yours begin to long for change? Because your Father alone knows your heart and knows when it is turned toward Him.

Transformed through His Power

Awareness of His mercy toward me continually renews my heart and mind. More and more I want to thank Him and worship Him as the very strength of my life. My heart strives to live in and share in the wonder of His mercy. As Paul urged the Romans:

> *In view of God's mercy...offer your bodies as living sacrifices, holy and pleasing to God—this is your spiritual act of worship. Do not conform any longer to the pattern of this world, but be transformed by the renewing of your mind. Then you will be able to test and approve what God's will is—His good, pleasing and perfect will.*
>
> (Romans 12:1–2)

The more time you spend in the Word, learning from God, the more your mind is transformed and renewed. You begin to jump out of the thorns and hedges and onto the life path of the Remnant believer, because your mind is being made different by the Holy Spirit.

The will of God becomes pleasing to you. Your heart understands and accepts His will, because your mind is transformed. The very center of your being becomes empowered by His Word.

The Word will change your life. As you begin to worship Him with your heart and yield your body to Him, a new energy is released into your life. You will find that you are able to test all the teachings shot at you from the world, the flesh and the enemy.

Your spirit will never again be in harmony with what is not pleasing to God. The Holy Spirit replaces the spirits of deceit, hardness and confusion with His truth. You now thirst for fellowship with God and His people.

The transforming of your mind through His strength, and a desire to live in the blessings of God, will enable you to see the folly of the false teacher and the lies of those whose father is Satan. There is only one choice to make: following God or following Satan. There are no gray areas into which you can wander during your earthly life. You and I choose the God of Abraham,

Isaac, and Jacob by surrendering to Christ, or we bow down to Satan himself. Jesus Christ said, *"If God were your Father, you would love Me"* (John 8:42).

> *Why is My language not clear to you? Because you are unable to hear what I say. You belong to your father, the devil, and you want to carry out your father's desire. He was a murderer from the beginning, not holding to the truth, for there is no truth in him. When he lies, he speaks his native language, for he is a liar and the father of lies.*
>
> (John 8:43–44)

And so we clearly know who has sold a failing, stumbling moral code to our communities, nations, and world. Certainly it has not come from the God we read about in Psalm 78, who gives us explicit instructions for life.

The reality is that God allows us to choose life or death. When I hear a person with a rebellious or hardened heart claim, "I prayed about it and feel some sin is all right," I can see there is a broken life road ahead. There always is. One of God's great attributes is that we can trust Him. If He cannot trust us, we are outside of His created design. You cannot build a loving, trustworthy relationship with anyone who walks outside the will of God.

The lost, rebellious, and hurting unbeliever today has bought into a lie that will never result in a satisfied, harmonious and peaceful life. Often the results of a flesh or world relationship are very painful. The results are felt through the next generation. Your own children may come to you seeking abortions at age 13. A new generation may give into the cravings for drugs, alcohol, or other addictions. A family without harmony or love for one another will live in bondage, never in triumph.

"It runs in the family" is a common phrase. Has your family history repeated itself generation after generation? As in the history of earlier generations, *"like their fathers they* [are] *disloyal and faithless"* (Psalm 78:57).

This Message Is the Same

Psalm 78 was written in the tenth century before Christ. In the first century in the Year of the Lord, Christ's powerful apostle Paul encountered the ascended Savior and became a Remnant believer. In covenant relationship, Paul was committed to teaching the generations how to live daily as true believers. He wrote God's same message to the Corinthian church about an obedient lifestyle:

> *Do you not know that the wicked will not inherit the kingdom of God? Do not be deceived: Neither the sexually immoral nor idolaters nor adulterers nor male prostitutes nor homosexual offenders nor thieves nor the greedy nor drunkards nor slanderers nor swindlers will inherit the kingdom of God.* (1 Corinthians 6:9–10)

"Do you not know?" Paul asks. Of course, there are those who actually do not know, because their parents and the generations before them never taught the Word of God, the history of God, and most of all, the great love God has for His children. That is now the Remnant work of the true lovers of God.

God is your engine and is much more powerful within you than an F-16 United States military jet. For the past several years, I have often been privileged to share and teach at several United States Air Force bases in Europe. In the early morning, I have been awakened by the sound of powerful, screaming jets racing down a runway and lifting into the skies.

It's an exhilarating sound that touches my heart because of what an Air Force officer's wife, Christy, D.E.W.W.'s European Coordinator, shared with me one morning. I asked her if the sound itself bothered her so early every morning. She said no, because everyone there knew that sound was "the sound of freedom!" Since then I eagerly anticipate hearing those jets roaring off in the morning and the reassuring sound of them returning every night.

Those sounds remind me to thank God that our nation has a powerful and protective Air Force keeping us safe. Ministering in many different post-Soviet countries after the 1989 revolutions and visiting the former concentration camps of the Nazi regime, I have seen the horrors of the loss of freedom. I have seen firsthand the legacy a dictator has left in Romania, destroying the land and the lives of a beautiful people.

That "sound of freedom" means that the hand of the Lord has blessed our nation with His protection through the United States Air Force. May those who lead within it be covenant keepers, and let us pray for those who are protecting us.

Empowering your life can be compared to experiencing the liftoff and flight of the F-16. Of course, as I have said before, it is a matter of choice. Why would you or I or anyone deliberately try to fly through life's years on self-power or with false gods? This choice is as blind as a decision to lift an F-16 off the ground with bicycle pedals.

I personally know and have witnessed the marvelous life changes that take place when a person experiences His power. No wonder Satan tries so hard to close human ears to the offers of Almighty God. You must take the first step, which is the desire to change and give your life to God Jesus Christ. Next, God the Holy Spirit will begin to open your eyes, ears, mind, and heart so that you will trust God and love His ways.

Walking with Christ is exciting and full of freedom. I see His glorious work, His provision, His corrections, His mercy, and His forgiveness in my life daily. Psalm 78 has special meaning to me, because I recall the times when I was just as rebellious as the people of the Exodus in the desert. I certainly have experienced deliverance and a changed heart by God loving me enough to forgive me.

When I live in His mercy and His grace, He focuses my eyes back on Him when I am discouraged. His grace is the unmerited favor He grants to me as a believing Christian. According to Vine, grace describes God's attitude toward me as a law-breaker and rebel.[6]

His forgiveness has taught me that I am in process. When I rebel or try to rely on myself, I experience His corrections, and sometimes they can be painful. Actually, they mostly are quite gentle, but my heart must be in the right condition to recognize the Holy Spirit redirecting my steps. Otherwise, I set myself up for a bit more attention-getting correction.

Interestingly, in life, we cannot hide our hearts from God. He knows my heart and my motives, as He knows yours. Once you accept this fact, you begin to hear the gentle whispers of God. You can then experience new freedom in Him.

Wild and Futile Religious Dance

I have found that the heart response of some can be vicious, as recorded in the Old Testament.

Jezebel, which means "where is Baal," had a heart that did not follow the God of Abraham, Isaac, and Jacob. She turned all her vicious fury upon the prophet Elijah. Dark spirits of the gods she worshipped screamed in her mind, because they could not overpower the strength God demonstrated through His Remnant man, Elijah.

Jezebel was the daughter of the Sidonite King Ethbaal, which means "Baal is alive," and the wife of Israel's evil King Ahab. King Ahab (874–853 B.C.) allowed Jezebel to zealously introduce Baal worship to the Northern Kingdom of Israel. Baal was to be officially worshipped alongside God (Yahweh). The Remnant prophet Elijah mightily opposed this evil. God enabled Elijah to reveal His absolute power. This led to direct confrontation with Jezebel's prophets of Baal.

Elijah warned that a person cannot worship two gods. There is only one omniscient and omnipotent God. Has much changed today?

Look at the past months of your life and the lives of those with whom you are in close relationship. What and who do you worship? That will be the center of your conversations, your priority goals. It will take up the largest amount of your mental and emotional energy.

How many professing Christians choose persecutors of the faith as partners? Anyone who is not in covenant with the one holy God is a persecutor.

God demonstrated that His words through Elijah were truth. On Mount Carmel the evil prophets and King Ahab were challenged to prove that the gods Baal and Asherah had supreme power. Yahweh, the omnipotent God, not only exhibited His absolute supremacy and power, but killed the false prophets (1 Kings 18:1–40).

The author of Ecclesiastes said in great wisdom:

What has been will be again, what has been done will be done again; there is nothing new under the sun.

(Ecclesiastes 1:9)

We experience great mercy in His covenant relationship. God is faithful in His mercy in spite of our rebellious ways. He enables the Remnant to live in triumph.

What is meant by the mercy *(Gr. eleos)* of God? Mercy is the act of God; peace is the resulting experience in the heart of man.[7] Mercy *(Gr. eleeo)* means, in general, to feel sympathy with the misery of another, and especially sympathy manifested in action.[8] The mercy of God is acted out in His love, when we are in need of spiritual strengthening or correction. God has always granted mercy to His Remnant.

Knowing Him through His Word and through experience is personal. Please believe that the Cross of Jesus was for the world, and that world is you. As closely as you hold your own child and listen intently to the precious words your child speaks, the Lord God holds you even more closely. Never, never listen to or believe anything different.

How deeply hurt the nail-pierced Savior must be when a professing believer claims that God is much too busy to be bothered with the least little detail or need of his or her life. If that were true, Christ could have had a supervisory, distant relationship without paying for our sin through His agony on the Cross.

The prophet Elijah called out to the people, *"How long will you waver between two opinions? If the Lord is God, follow Him; but if Baal is God, follow him"* (1 Kings 18:21). "Waver" to the Hebrews meant "dance." The wild and futile dances of pagan rituals were intended to arouse the pagan gods. Many in the world around us are performing futile dances today. Religions who have made gods of man through non-biblical rules or wild and frenzied practices may have the same question asked of them.

God desires to have an intimate relationship with each of His covenant people. He continues to gather a Remnant people and makes it possible through Christ for you and me to be in covenant relationship with Him.

Notes

1. Vine, *Vine's Expository Dictionary,* pp. 60–61.

2. Guralink, *Webster's New World Dictionary,* p. 331.

3. L. Trammell, interview by author, 1996. Used with permission.

4. L. Trammell, *The Highest Calling of All—God's Ultimate Purpose for Each of Us* (Duluth, GA: Ablaze Publishing, 1991), p. 9.

5. Unger, *Unger's Bible Dictionary,* p. 624.

6. Vine, *Vine's Expository Dictionary,* p. 61.

7. Ibid.

8. Ibid.

Chapter 10

Triumph and Action

Triumph

S et apart your heart for the Lord. Begin to experience the mighty rest He gives you. Caution—if you have been giving God a low priority in your life, your intellect may tell you that experiencing God will mean denying pleasure. Dark forces have tricked the mind of mankind since the Garden of Eden. From the time of the Garden, as we have seen, man has chosen to open his mind to accept the lie.

I hope that this book has presented an overview of God's plan for man. The relationship with His beloved creation is a covenant relationship.

I do not think that we as human beings can ever grasp the full scope of God's poured-out, divine love. Usually, we define His love by our own ability to love or by the way we perceive that humans may or may not meet our needs for affirmation, loyalty, trust, and faithfulness.

The apostle Paul recognized that prayer was necessary for you and me, so we may have power to comprehend with all the saints what is the breadth and length and height and depth of the great love of Christ (Ephesians 3:18). If you should be tempted to think that you can live triumphantly on your own mere humanity, I suggest you earnestly talk with God, asking the Holy Spirit to protect your mind and heart.

Of course, if you have never chosen the great life in Christ, your mind loves to worship at the altar of man. From the time the serpent appeared to deceive Eve, and she and Adam bought the lie, the serpent has continued to crawl through minds for thousands of years. Satan attacks the mind of both the believer (2 Corinthians 11:3) and the unbeliever (2 Corinthians 4:3–4).

God, as we can read in the book of Genesis, created the world with a plan for man and woman to live triumphantly. His design was for His creation to live without want and without knowledge of evil. Man chose knowledge of evil, and evil deceives. It is like the drug dealer who introduces a child or adult to cocaine by telling them that it feels great and they will be able to experience new heights. The resulting fall and bleak future is not acknowledged, of course.

The enemy of God, Satan, works in the human mind. "The Word of God has shown you that the prince of this world works against our hearts and minds to deceive, destroy, slander and justify evil choices. His goal is to hurt God and avoid his destiny."[1]

The Bible is without a doubt the greatest story ever told. The Bible, I believe, is truth. The greatest lie we have been told is that true joy is found in sin. Sin is anything outside the will of God. Beloved of God, is your perception of living a Remnant life one in which you will live less of a life? Choose triumphant life!

Wonderful news! When your heart begins to yearn for the presence of God, refreshing waters of truth transform your mind. Experiencing the presence of God becomes a wonder as your mind begins to bind to the mind of Jesus Christ. In the midst of trials and temptations, you will find the Holy Spirit comforting you, the Father protecting you, and Jesus providing in ways you cannot conceive.

Your heart now yearns to choose His moral laws. The Old Testament commandments will be written on your heart as a keeper of Christ's New Covenant. New thoughts now become new action.

Action Steps for Triumphant Living

FIRST, *PUT OFF THE OLD NATURE*

1. Put to death what is earthly in you: fornication, impurity, passion, evil desire, and covetousness, which is idolatry.
2. Although you once walked in these ways, put them all away: anger, wrath, malice, slander and foul talk from your mouth.
3. Do not lie to one another, because you have put off the old nature.

Colossians 3:1–9 (RSV)

SECOND, *PUT ON YOUR NEW NATURE*

1. Put on the new nature which is being renewed and is in His image.
2. Put on, chosen one, compassion, kindness, lowliness, meekness and patience.
3. Forbear one another; forgive your complaint against another. As the Lord has forgiven you, so you also must forgive.
4. Put on love, which binds everything together in perfect harmony.

5. Allow the peace of Christ to rule in your heart. Believers are to be of one body.
6. Be thankful.
7. Let the Word of Christ dwell in you richly!
8. Teach and admonish one another in all wisdom.
9. Sing psalms and hymns and spiritual songs with thankful hearts.
10. And whatever you do, in word or deed, do everything in the name of the Lord Jesus, giving thanks to God the Father through Him. Whatever your task, work heartily, as serving the Lord and not men.

Colossians 3:10–17, 23 (RSV)

You can triumphantly "put off" your old heart and mind like an old garment and "put on" new garments. Wearing your old thoughts and emotions are like wearing grave clothes.

Lazarus was raised from the dead by Jesus Christ (John 11:3–44) for us to see His power, and to raise us from living in death to living in triumph. After commanding that the stone be removed that blocked Lazarus from the light of life, Jesus told him to take action. *"Lazarus, come out!"* (John 11:43).

Lazarus took action and came to Jesus, but there was yet another command. Jesus instructed, *"Take off the grave clothes"* (John 11:44). Grave clothes were the linens that tightly wrapped a dead body. Then all could see Lazarus was now living, and he could rejoice. Lazarus experienced new life and lived out the rest of his days without the decaying grave clothes.

You are called by Jesus to the same life in His image and in His power. You must take action! If you insist on staying wrapped in the old-life grave clothes, you will never walk in freedom. Faith in God means believing Him as Lazarus did. Walk out, and put off the old nature's grave clothes. Leave the darkness of your spiritual grave.

Putting off my old nature has been a lifelong process. Some old habits have been broken off in a moment. With others, it seems, I take two steps forward and one step backward. From life as a self-sufficient atheist to a new believer to a life committed to serve Him, I have had to prayerfully ask Him to lead me to obedience:

> *Conduct yourselves wisely toward outsiders, making the most of the time. Let your speech always be gracious, seasoned with salt, so that you may know how you ought to answer every one.* (Colossians 4:5–6 RSV)

Our answers must come directly from God's Word. He speaks to you through His Word. God is willing to forgive you even when you hold onto some cherished parts of your old nature. It takes times of truly experiencing the Lord's deliverance to accept that we are free of an old-nature behavior. He heals.

I have found that I have held onto a part of my old nature, because I am very comfortable with it. Each of us has particular personal choices we make over and over with disastrous results. Often, God allows us to stumble about until we realize it doesn't work for us, and we begin to listen to His voice.

At that point we cry out for God's help, telling Him we are weary of failing and are not strong enough to change or to even want to change. The Holy Spirit will then change our hearts, and we will begin to yield to God's way. Just as He has heard the cry of the Remnant throughout time, He hears us now. He forgives us, and He alone delivers us. Living triumphantly means giving up all attempts to be strong in our own strength. What a glorious God to both forgive us and deliver us!

You can live life in peace and harmony and have new purpose. God's Word is written for you personally. Taking a new route means you will experience some refreshing views, you will have safety on the slippery roads, and you will be comforted on life's bumpy highway. The Remnant triumphs over all circumstances.

Answers are available. God does not give you directions, such as the Ten Commandments given on Mount Sinai to Moses, or the directions given to Paul for the Colossians, unless He knows you are absolutely capable of living them. God is clear. You, your family, your community, and your nation have a set of values, behaviors, responses, and attitudes that are clearly stated for triumphant life. What values, behaviors, and attitudes do you believe in? If you have made up your mind, it is time to seek God. Ask Jesus to give you a new heart. Seek God, repent, and find real life.

As surely as God put the stars, moon, and sun in such perfect order, and created waterfalls, trees, and majestic mountains on this earth, He knows what is best for you and me. When you believe God for your moment-by-moment life, it is going to be a powerful transformation. Pray, as Paul counseled in Colossians 4:2 (RSV): *"Continue steadfastly in prayer, being watchful in it with thanksgiving."*

Ask God, in the name of Jesus Christ, to put off your old life and to clothe your heart and mind anew in the righteous garments of Christ. Thank Him from your heart for the joys of triumph. Thank Him for the victory in Christ, over the hold that Satan has had on you in any of the areas listed in the book of Colossians as those to be put off.

- Praise His holy name for giving you the power to travel the triumphant highway.
- Confess to Him all the "old nature" worship to which you cling.
- Seek His face alone as you confess your love of any ways of your old nature.

- Take His hand in yours and share how you believed only in your own strength. If you feel He will not forgive the ugly sins, the deep inner sins of envy, greed, or impurity, tell Him. He will!

We all need a heart change in some of these areas. Not only must we repent of the sins of the old nature, but we must choose to put on the actions of the new nature as commanded in Colossians 3 and 4.

He already knows everything about you. Only He knows your innermost thoughts and deeds in the darkness. He wants your trust. A deeply intimate and committed relationship involves trust when living out a covenant both parties have agreed to keep. Jesus Christ will set you free!

Notes

1. P. D. Fritz, *The Love That Lasts I* (Reno, NV: D.E.W.W. Ministry, 1991), Book 3, p. 8.

Chapter 11

Search No More

You never need stand at the grave of your life and weep. We have God's promise:

> *Fear not, for I have redeemed you; I have summoned you by name....You are precious and honored in My sight, and...I love you.* (Isaiah 43:1, 4)

God is sovereign and has given man rules so that he may live triumphantly. God's will is perfect, the will to love you and bless you. The Remnant is God's treasured possession, and His blessings pour out to His people.

The Remnant are people set apart for God. The numbers are known only to God. It could be few, or it could be billions. The Remnant is not determined by man's opinions, denominations, or religious affiliations. The Remnant are those who will be gathered to God for eternity. He has promised to gather the Remnant.

A Remnant is a faithful follower, a believer through Jesus Christ, who lives in covenant relationship. God's covenant relationship is a two-way agreement.

We need not walk through a lifetime on earth without knowing who we are. No one should stand at your grave and conclude, as Willie Loman's son did, that you never knew who you were. At this moment, do you know?

God has promised new life through Jesus Christ, His Son. His death and resurrection are a reality. The Father has given you an unconditional promise, that if you believe in Him and surrender your life to the outstretched arms of Jesus Christ, you have eternal life (Romans 10:9–10).

If you have any questions about your personal salvation, please write to me, Priscilla Fritz, D.E.W.W. Ministry, P.O. Box 18370, Reno, Nevada 89511 U.S.A. Please write if you have any questions at all.

Acceptance of God the Father, Son, and Holy Spirit guarantees you life in the promises of God. Changed and new, you have the power to live a new life as God gives you a heart to love Him.

God has kept His promise to man and woman, because a faithful Remnant has always obeyed God. Others will know that He is the only God by His faithfulness to the covenant keeper.

From the Garden of Eden to this day, man has rebelled against God and lived in unbelief. Yet God has not turned His back on the people He created. He has promised to gather the Remnant to Himself, and God would be known as a liar if He abandoned mankind to its own destruction. All people will know He is the Alpha and Omega and the only true God by His faithfulness.

In God's time line, the length of time from the Garden creation of man to this moment is but a heartbeat. All of our lives throughout time are closely linked together. There is no difference between you and your circumstances and those of Abraham, Moses, the Israelites, kings, and first-century people.

Does God ever reject His own? Paul asked the same question. *"Did God reject His people? By no means!...God did not*

reject His people, whom He foreknew" (Romans 11:1–2). His
people are the Remnant. The Remnant can trust God. A Remnant will be saved, as God promises in Romans 9:27 (RSV).

God will gather His people together on the day of the Lord
Jesus Christ's return. The Remnant can look forward to the future great assembly. Remnant believers will rejoice and praise
God the Father, Son, and Holy Spirit. This gathering will take
place at His throne, and I pray that you, beloved reader, will be
there. The choice is yours. Do not be misled into thinking that
any religious act or that attending church will get you there.
There are probably only a few of the Remnant in any given
Christian church. The covenant keepers are steadfast believers
who have a heart of obedience to God, whom they love.

With a mighty word, God created the earth and everything
in it. He created a universe of planets and stars in perfect bal-
ance and order. God spoke, and man and woman were created
for Him to divinely love and for them to return that love. That
love is to be walked out in intimacy, trust, and in a covenant between God and man. The covenant promises His protection,
care, and blessing, providing we are faithful.

He had you on His mind when He created life. He wanted to
walk with you in a great expression of love, the depth of which
we cannot comprehend with the human mind.

The Bible, in both the Old and New Testaments, records the
covenant agreements God entered into with His people. The
people of Israel and of the world have continually failed to walk
in obedience and loyalty to God. God's forgiveness and His discipline shows us time and again the depth of His love. The
promises of God are made to the obedient, faithful Remnant.
Obedience is not a matter of deprivation. It is a pleasure to love
God.

Because God is holy, rebellion and disobedience are not allowed in His presence. The great sins of His people were idol

worship, compromising God, and failure to obey the laws. He was specific in His guidance, and the sin nature of man chose to exalt itself. So great and continual was the rebellion of man that His wrath was poured out upon them. The people to whom God had given the Promised Land were loved but corrected by Him. Rebellion is not acceptable to God. He is holy, and sin causes Him anger.

So persistent was the rebellion of the people of the promise that they did not keep the Kingdom of Israel together. The sin of both the kings and the people led to the division of the land into Judah and Israel. Their disobedience opened the door to Israel's defeat by the Assyrians and the Babylonians.

Our actions as a Church and as individuals bring the same wrath of God upon ourselves. He is a covenant keeper, incapable of a lie. He will be faithful today when we are not, but He will not allow sin in His presence.

God's wrath allowed the Assyrians and Babylonians to defeat and destroy Israel, including the sacred city of Jerusalem. He gave the enemy the power to destroy. He warned and warned Israel, just as an exasperated parent does. The Remnant was faithful, and He did not turn His back on His promise to Abraham and David to keep and continue His people. He warns and disciplines nations and individuals today.

The people of the promise knew of the great powerful deliverance of God from the past generations. History was taught in the oral tradition, in the homes, and down through the generations. We have full access to the wonders of God as well. Not only do we have the teachings of God passed down through the generations, we have the written Word, the Bible. History also verifies biblical fact. Unbelievers, especially, have tried to disprove the facts of the Bible with the most dedicated and scientific search. Even as more discoveries are made in the world system today, the truth of the Bible still has never been proved false. In fact, the opposite has happened. The Bible has been found to be true.

God has made Himself known to you. God is Truth, and He does not change. God will gather the Remnant to Himself. We are to live our lives according to His moral laws and in His will. There is a plan. Jesus will return and rule His beloved forever. No other gods will come for you or will save you. From the beginning, God has offered men and women and children real life. From the beginning, nothing has changed. Many have rebelled, but the Remnant has been faithful:

> *Now all has been heard; here is the conclusion of the matter: Fear God and keep His commandments, for this is the whole duty of man. For God will bring every deed into judgment, including every hidden thing, whether it is good or evil.* (Ecclesiastes 12:13–14)

Reverence God, and worship Him only. You will find that He will never fail you. Your life will become new, restored, refreshed, and as glorious as the sunrise over the Red Sea. By His grace, by favor undeserved, God parts the sea before you as well. There are no obstacles, because Christ is your power. If there is anything holding you back, ask God right now for the power to live in triumph.

Enter into covenant relationship with God and live in triumph from this day forward. Remnant life is triumphant life. May you and I meet at the throne of our Father and rejoice forever!

Unlike Willie Loman's son, others will never need to say you did not know who you were.

> *So too, at the present time there is a Remnant chosen by grace.* (Romans 11:5)